Y0-DYO-355

The United States in the Supreme War Council

The United States in the Supreme War Council

AMERICAN WAR AIMS AND INTER-ALLIED STRATEGY, 1917–1918

By DAVID F. TRASK

Wesleyan University Press : MIDDLETOWN : CONNECTICUT

Library of Congress Catalog Card Number: 61-14237
Manufactured in the United States of America
First Edition

In memory of my father, Hugh A. Trask (1896-1952),
a member of the American Expeditionary Forces
during World War I.

Table of Contents

Preface

In recent years Americans have become increasingly interested in the history of warfare, a rather grim commentary on the omnipresence of international tensions. Many studies of the Civil War and World War II have appeared, and historians have also explored anew the War of 1812, the Spanish-American War, and World War I. The First World War has assumed a special significance because it was the root of many problems which now engage our interest. It opened the floodgates to totalitarianism, not only in Germany but in Russia and Italy as well. It represented a revival and expansion of coalition warfare on an even larger scale than during the Napoleonic era. It posed the possibility of maintaining international peace by collective security rather than by the seemingly obsolete balance of power. It destroyed the confident assumption that democracy would inevitably encompass all the nations of the world and thus guarantee universal peace and justice.

Most scholars who have studied American participation in World War I have concentrated either upon the neutrality which preceded the American declaration of war on 6 April 1917 or upon the peacemaking which followed the Armistice of 11 November 1918. Few have concerned themselves with the warfare which divided the prewar and postwar phases of the American involvement. This neglect is understandable. Disillusionment with the Versailles settlement naturally centered interest upon either explanations of the process by which the United States became a belligerent or analyses of the process by which the peace was lost. Today we possess the perspectives created by the Second World War and the Cold War, as well as a large body of only partially exploited data concerning American belligerency during World War I. It is now possible to restudy the events of 1917 and 1918, drawing upon these new perspectives and materials. From the many aspects of the war years which invite new researches, the author has chosen to examine one of the least discussed and most significant facets of American belligerency, the relationship between the military decisions of the American government and the fundamental war aims espoused by President Woodrow Wilson.

This book considers the relationships between American diplomatic and military decisions during the decisive phase of World War I. It is an analysis of the American association with the Entente Powers—Great Britain, France, and Italy—after the United States finally entered the great struggle. The American relationship with the Entente Powers was not formalized by an official alliance, but it was no less real in its consequences within the United States government. To ignore this reality is to miss perhaps the most significant aspect of America's role in the defeat of the Central Powers. The inter-Allied perspective of this study yields new interpretations or revisions of older views. Historians must reconsider the common assumption that the development and implementation of American policy and strategy during World War I was generally haphazard. They must also reassess the widely held belief that President Wilson and his associates did not appreciate the significance of military strategy and its relation to the consummation of war aims. To examine these and similar questions, the author has concentrated on the procedures by which the Allied and Associated Powers coordinated political-military plans during 1918.

The instrument of inter-Allied cooperation was an organization called the Supreme War Council. It came into existence after the disastrous events of 1917, a most important but curiously obscure institution. It was composed of the prime ministers of Britain, France, and Italy, or their deputies, along with the President of the United States or his deputy. One other representative from each country, usually the foreign minister, also participated in the deliberations of the group. Meeting regularly during 1918, the Supreme War Council discussed and helped to shape over-all political-military strategy of the western coalition. Its history throws new light on the nature of President Wilson's wartime preparations for the peace settlement which he hoped would make the world safe for democracy. This study therefore traces the development of the Supreme War Council in terms of the participation of the United States in its deliberations, thus emphasizing the generally accepted but frequently neglected maxim that political-military decisions of nations engaged in coalition warfare are consequences of adjustments to the aspirations and interests of allies as well as of enemies.

Thanks are due to the staffs of the several libraries mentioned in the bibliography, as well as to those individuals who kindly extended permission to examine the manuscript collections listed in the same place. The author wishes also to note the professional counsel rendered by his colleagues at Wesleyan University, especially Professors Samuel Hugh Brockunier and Carl E. Schorske (now of the University of California). Above all, he takes pride in acknowledging the guidance of Professor Ernest R. May, Harvard University, who first drew his interest to the First World War and guided his early researches, and he desires to recognize the unfailing loyalty and gentle criticism of his wife, Roberta Kirsch Trask.

Middletown, Connecticut D. F. T.
July 1961

The United States in the Supreme War Council

CHAPTER 1

American Intervention in World War I

One of the most striking characteristics of modern warfare is its cooperative nature. Twentieth-century wars have usually been waged by opposing coalitions—by allied nations struggling against another group of sovereign states. In our time, war, the most imposing manifestation of the competitive propensities of humanity, requires a remarkable degree of cooperation among the nations who compose given military coalitions. Nevertheless, the most cursory glance at the history of war demonstrates that military partnerships are often quite unstable. Napoleon supposedly preferred to engage coalitions rather than individual nations, convinced that the throes of cooperation seriously weakened his adversaries.

Cooperation among allies is difficult to achieve and sustain because the nations who compose given coalitions rarely fight for exactly the same purposes. Although the members of a coalition may be joined by antagonism toward a common enemy, they often disagree on the proper strategy to defeat that enemy. Although interallied controversies develop from many sources of irritation, the most important cause usually is divergence in political aims.

World War I is a typical example of coalition warfare. Both the Western Powers and the Central Powers encountered many problems of cooperation as each alliance attempted to concert grand strategy and policy against the other. The Central Powers had less difficulty than the Western Powers, primarily because Germany exercised a profound superiority over her allies—Austria-Hungary, Bulgaria, and Turkey. The widely differing aims of the Entente Powers—Great Britain, France, Italy, and Russia—bred exceedingly complicated differences of opinion on matters of strategy, a circumstance which clearly vitiated the effectiveness of the coalition.

By April 1917, when the United States finally entered the struggle in association with the Entente Powers, the need for enhanced interallied cooperation within the Western coalition was already painfully apparent. During the rest of that year a series of disastrous military and political defeats, most of them at least partially attributable to a lack of inter-Allied coordination, finally convinced the Entente leaders of the need for more effective methods of consultation and cooperation in matters of strategy and policy. Fearful of a massive German offensive in France designed to end the war in 1918, the Western Powers finally set up a Supreme War Council to engender and sustain inter-Allied cooperation against the common enemy. This organization was created at Rapallo, Italy, on 7 November 1917. Shortly after its founding, the United States became a member of the Supreme War Council. The new institution brought together the heads of the governments of the principal Allied and Associated Powers (with the exception of Russia) in order to "watch over the general conduct of the war" and insure a "better coordination of military action."[1] A board of Permanent Military Representatives, made up of one distinguished soldier from each member nation, was created in order to provide professional military counsel.

This study of United States policy and strategy during 1917-1918 concentrates particularly on American dealings with the Supreme War Council.[2] Since the nation was deeply involved in a military coalition, it is most important to treat the development of American policy and strategy in the light of the pressures engendered by the need to act in concert with the Entente Powers. Any other approach to American policy and strategy during World War I inevitably produces serious distortions. This special design incidentally casts light on the general characteristics of inter-Allied cooperation during the concluding year of World War I.

The war aims and peace plans contemplated by the American government diverged considerably from those projected by her European "associates." At the outset of American belligerency—seven months before the establishment of the Supreme War Council—President Wilson and his closest advisors had begun to outline the war aims and peace plans of the United States. During the same period —in conjunction with this effort—the American government made fundamentally important decisions concerning the use of American military strength against the Central Powers. These actions vitally influenced relations with the Entente Powers when the United States entered into the inter-Allied political-military consultations conducted at meetings of the Supreme War Council. In fact, these early decisions governed the nature of American dealings with the Entente Powers throughout the remaining year of the war, when the task of coordinating inter-Allied policy and strategy was assumed by the Supreme War Council. For this reason these early decisions concerning policy and strategy, arrived at during the period April-November 1917, must be discussed in some detail before turning to the history of American relations with the Council.

AMERICAN WAR AIMS IN 1917

Early in January 1917, President Wilson told Colonel House: "This country does not intend to become involved in this war. . . . It would be a crime against civilization for us to go in."[3] Three months later he asked the Congress to declare war on Germany and attempted to justify participation in the holocaust he so desperately had tried to avoid. "It is a fearful thing," he said, "to lead this great peaceful people into war, into the most terrible and disastrous of all wars, civilization itself seeming to be in the balance." The American motive would not be revenge, but rather the "vindication of right, of human right." To this end the United States accepted the gage of battle:

> The right is more precious than peace, and we shall fight for the things we have always carried nearest our hearts,—for democracy, for the right of those who submit to authority to have a voice in their own Governments, for the rights and liberties of small nations, for a universal dominion of right by such a concert of free peoples as shall bring peace and safety to all nations and make the world itself at last free.[4]

Thus Woodrow Wilson dedicated himself and his countrymen to the building of a new order of peace and justice. Throughout the great war and the postwar peace conference he struggled to fulfill his grand design—a massive moral design—by political action.[5]

The President announced that the nation would "exert all its power and employ all its resources to bring the Government of the German Empire to terms and end the war." The struggle would be waged cooperatively with other democracies across the seas, including Russia, so recently emancipated from autocratic domination by revolutionary means. The war would require "the utmost practicable cooperation in counsel and action with the governments now at war with Germany." Financial credits, material resources, naval support, and a great army—all would be mobilized to destroy the enemy and clear the path to that "universal dominion of right" envisioned by the war leader.[6]

Thus the political-military intentions of the United States were clearly—if very generally—exposed to the world. The President did not specify the details of that future dominion of right, nor did he elaborate the military plans of the nation. The reason for these omissions, aside from security, was simple enough; the government had not as yet developed detailed political-military plans. A general outlook had been announced, but the means of implementation were still in abeyance.

The United States entered the war without striking prior bargains with the Entente as Italy had done in 1915. President Wilson committed the nation with evident purposes in mind, and these he adumbrated with surpassing eloquence. He pronounced them unilaterally without diplomatic reference to the Entente—without consultation and agreement.[7] The President feared that his intended program would sow seeds of suspicion, thus inhibiting coordinated action against the Germans. After his war message the President eschewed public comments on war aims as well as official conversations with the "Associates"—his designation for the Entente Powers.[8] Writing to Colonel House after some three months of war, the President epitomized his reasons for avoiding discussions of war aims:

> *England and France have not the same views with regard to peace that we have* by any means. When the war is over we can force them to our way of thinking because by that time they will, among other things, be financially in our hands: but we cannot force them now, and any attempt to speak for them or to our common mind would

> bring on disagreements which would inevitably come to the surface in public and rob the whole thing of its effect.
>
> Our real peace terms,—those upon which we shall undoubtedly insist, are not now acceptable to either France or Italy (leaving Great Britain for the moment out of consideration).[9]

Clearly the President was under no illusions concerning the war aims of the Entente Powers. He sought to adjourn discussion of the peace settlement until the Central Powers had been defeated and American power greatly enhanced. The American government adhered to this policy throughout most of 1917 until changing conditions dictated a new departure.[10]

Although President Wilson couched American war aims in general terms to avoid wrangles with the Entente Powers, he assiduously concerned himself with the problems of the peace settlement. To assist in preparing data he constituted the "Inquiry," a group of experts on international affairs, under the direction of Colonel House.[11] He was determined to sustain his capacity to insure an enlightened peace. If necessary, he would dictate a just settlement.

AMERICAN MILITARY PREPARATIONS IN 1917

The United States was unprepared for war. After the diplomatic break with Germany early in February 1917, the War Department began to consider the problems of organizing a sizable army. Lack of information and inadequate personnel on the General Staff greatly limited these activities. On 5 March the War Department presented a a plan to the President providing for the mobilization and training of 500,000 men within six months. On 29 March Secretary of War Newton D. Baker recommended enlarging the Regular Army and the National Guard and proposed a selective draft to provide another 1,000,000 men.[12]

Despite these preliminaries, the President's military advisors assumed that the United States would concentrate on assisting the Entente Powers with materials, shipping, naval support, and financial aid but would not place a large army in the field. American planners hoped to enhance the effectiveness of the Allies by insuring that the national mobilization did not interfere with European logistical needs. Colonel House summed up the prevailing mood: "No one looks with favor upon our raising a large army at the moment, believing it would be better if we permit volunteers to enlist in the Allied armies."[13]

Early in April the War Department decided to prepare a large force, but the General Staff planned to hold these troops in the United States until at least a million were ready for combat. They were to be reserved for decisive operations against Germany.[14] No one seems to have anticipated the eventual size of the American mobilization, largely because the Entente initially did not ask for extensive manpower.[15] The War Department's decision to field a force of at least a million men preceded widespread recognition that the troops would be needed in France.[16]

Shortly after the American entry, the Allies sent missions to Washington, principally to welcome the United States into the conflict and to make preliminary arrangements for extensive cooperation. Their arrival stimulated a searching consideration of the American military program. The most important missions were the Balfour group from Britain and the Viviani group from France. Two distinguished soldiers, General Tom Bridges for the British and Marshal Joseph Joffre for the French, initiated staff conversations with Secretary of War Baker and his principal military colleagues, General Hugh Scott, the Chief of Staff, and his deputy, General Tasker Bliss.

Bridges unexpectedly proposed that the United States rapidly mobilize 500,000 men and ship them immediately to Europe. There the British would equip and train them, preparatory to their use as replacements in depleted British formations.[17] This proposal was the first of many which urged the "amalgamation" of American troops into Entente armies by small or intermediate-sized units. The men would then come under the command of European officers. Joffre did not suggest amalgamation at the outset, saying that "it was bad to divide an army." Instead he urged the Americans to train a large force in order to fight independently on the Western Front in conjunction with the French.[18] But soon he altered his views and began to recommend amalgamation.[19] Both Joffre and Bridges requested an early dispatch of a token American force to France in order to "show the flag" in Europe and stimulate morale prior to the principal reinforcement. The defeat of the combined Franco-British assault on the German Army in France during April and May 1917 altered European conceptions of American contributions to the inter-Allied effort.

These discussions brought about a series of far-reaching decisions by the American military leaders. The attitude of the missions confirmed Secretary Baker's original impression that a large American force would be needed in Europe. The first step was to authorize the shipment of a modest detachment from the Regular Army to France.[20] The War Department immediately and decisively opposed the schemes for amalgamation. General Bliss thought well of shipping raw troops to Europe for training, a policy which would hasten the American reinforcement, but he strongly deprecated amalgamation. By sending untrained troops but refusing to accept amalgamation, "we [the United States] could secure our proper and independent place on the line and not run the risk of having our organizations fed in here and there . . . thus losing our identity as a national army under our own control."[21] Secretary Baker assumed that the American army would operate primarily with the French because the Navy would naturally cooperate with the British. He believed public opinion would favor this policy. The sentimental attachment to France stemming from the tradition of Lafayette, coupled with the historic antagonism toward Great Britain, influenced this decision.[22]

After the missions departed, General Bliss summed up the attitude of the General Staff in a letter to Baker. At the root of his opinions was the belief that the United States should resist all proposals tending to interfere with the creation of an independent American army. Continuing to oppose amalgamation, he held that a disproportionate loss of American lives might occur without assurance that decisive results would be obtained. Bliss strongly suspected the Allies of deliberately seeking to interfere with the development of an independent American army. He said positively: "I do not believe our people would stand for it." Despite the urging of the missions, the General Staff still believed that the Entente should hold their lines until the American army could appear in France "to give the final, crushing blow."[23] This conclusion accorded with the program recommended by the War Department just before the arrival of the missions.[24]

These early discussions culminated in the dispatch of General John J. Pershing to France as commander-in-chief of the American Expeditionary Forces. Twelve thousand troops were sent to Europe immediately in order to cooperate with the French army.[25] Before his departure Pershing received orders clearly reflecting the current state of opinion in the War Department:

5. In military operations against the Imperial German Government you are directed to cooperate with the forces of the other countries employed against that enemy; but in so doing, the underlying idea must be kept in view that the forces of the United States are a separate and distinct component of the combined forces, the identity of which must be preserved. . . .

6. In general you are vested with all necessary authority to carry on the war vigorously in harmony with the spirit of these instructions and toward a victorious conclusion.[26]

These instructions indicated conclusively that when a large American army arrived in France it would operate independently in its own sector under its own commanders when sufficiently trained. Woodrow Wilson's determination "to bring the Government of the German Empire to terms and end the war" was beginning to acquire tangible military meaning.

Soon after his arrival in France, General Pershing began to press for a much larger army than previously discussed. His early estimate of the situation convinced him that the United States would have to contribute extensive military as well as naval and economic assistance. On 10 July 1917 he submitted a "General Organization Project" which called for 1,000,000 men by 1918, organized in twenty combat divisions. The over-all planning of the War Department, he thought, should contemplate a total force of some 3,000,000 men to be ready in two years.[27] This program was consolidated with a similar proposal presented by the War College. The "thirty-division plan" was the basis of the American mobilization until early in 1918.[28]

As time passed Pershing realized that the principal obstacle to a great American build-up was the scarcity of shipping. His memoirs record increasing anxiety and exasperation as sea transportation failed to materialize during the latter months of 1917.[29] The multiplication of Entente requests for material and even for unskilled workers increasingly irritated the General. Baker's comment to the President on Pershing's difficulties minced no words. "General Pershing," he wrote, "has reached the conclusion that the French would rather have us work for them than fight for them." The Secretary himself was "adhering rigidly to the policy of getting our own army organized."[30] The congenital American suspicion of Europe and Europe's ways continued to assert itself despite the exigencies of war. Pershing never altered his views. After a frightening series of Allied catastrophes, discussed in Chapter 2, Pershing reaffirmed the fundamental attitude he clung to tenaciously throughout the war:

> It seems clear to me that the war must be won on the Western Front, and that the efforts of the Allies should continue as now in progress, and that every possible energy that America can exert should be put forth there, whether the role is to be offensive or defensive.[31]

The American commander thus accepted the strategy of concentration on the Western Front which Britain and France had pursued since the early months of the war.

Unique conditions had prevailed on the Western Front following the First Battle of the Marne. The opposing armies were securely entrenched along a line extending from the North Sea to Switzerland. No expenditure of men and materials seemed capable of dislodging either force. Reacting to a long and futile series of failures to breach the German lines, many European observers began to advocate a new departure in strategy. The doctrine of the period held that the commander should concentrate his forces and direct them against the main body of the enemy in order to force a decision under favorable circumstances. The development of new weapons and tactics, however, had given the defense a powerful advantage. The critics of the doctrine of concentration maintained that the Allies should undertake operations in theaters other than France where their armies might fight a "war of movement" offering opportunities to eliminate certain of Germany's allies from the struggle. As frustrations and losses mounted along the Western Front, they advocated with increasing frequency campaigns against Austria-Hungary, Turkey, and Bulgaria. The proponents of operations in secondary theaters were known as "easterners," while those who held to the strategy of concentration in France were called "westerners."[32]

In September 1917 Secretary Baker ordered a study to estimate the feasibility of employing American troops in theaters other than the Western Front. Such operations were called "sideshows." Apparently this study was undertaken on the request of President Wilson.[33] Presumably he acted after receiving a letter from Prime Minister David Lloyd George of Great Britain, perhaps the most influential "easterner," which strongly urged a reconsideration of Allied strategy:

> For some time past, it has seemed to me that we ought to consider very carefully whether we cannot achieve decisive results by concentrating first against Germany's allies. . . . Today, the weakest part of the enemy's line is unquestionably the front of Germany's allies. They are weak not only militarily but politically. They are also very anxious for peace, so that a comparatively small success might produce far-reaching results.[34]

The War College Division of the General Staff busied itself with inquiries intended to fix the American attitude toward "sideshows."

In October, Secretary Baker gave the President a series of detailed memoranda which strongly defended the original American decision to concentrate military power in

France. One study, dealing with the fronts of Germany's allies, summed up the attitude of the War Department:

> The Western Front is nearest to us; it can be most readily reached and with the least danger; we there fight with England and France with whom we have the greatest natural interests; and we can make our power felt on that front quicker and stronger than anywhere else; and we are there opposed by Germany, who is our only real enemy.[35]

Clearly the War Department believed its decision to fight on the Western Front still remained valid. Neither the Secretary of War nor the President disputed this decision.[36] The combined planning of General Pershing in France and the General Staff in Washington envisioned a force of several million men to be concentrated in France for an offensive against the German army in accord with the time-honored precepts of concentration. The American army would operate independently under its own commanders within its own sector. There would be no turning back.

THE DISPATCH OF THE HOUSE MISSION TO EUROPE

During the summer and early fall of 1917 Colonel House began to receive intimations from Great Britain that the United States should take a larger part in inter-Allied consultations.[37] This pressure stemmed, among other things, from increasing concern over the military setbacks encountered by Anglo-French forces on the Western Front at this time. President Wilson, whose policy was determined by a profound wish to avoid embarrassing diplomatic entanglements, initially failed to respond to these hints. The official position of the American government was that the United States hesitated to contribute her counsel until her army had appeared in force on the Western Front. This explanation was a convenient excuse for retaining diplomatic independence.

As the urgency of the situation in Europe increased, Colonel House began to favor expanded American participation in inter-Allied discussions. In response to a message from Lloyd George, he urged the President to send Secretary of War Baker and Secretary of the Treasury William G. McAdoo to Europe for important consultations.[38] The British and the French, particularly aware of the need to concert activities in preparation for the campaign of 1918, were making plans for a great inter-Allied conference to meet in Paris during October. Formal invitations to the United States were sent by both France and Britain. In the face of mounting pressure, both from abroad and from Colonel House, the President's opposition weakened perceptibly.[39] Finally he decided to send Colonel House to Europe at the head of a formal mission to participate in the forthcoming Paris meetings.[40]

Sir William Wiseman, the ubiquitous liaison officer between Colonel House and the British government, exerted all of his considerable influence with the Colonel in order to bring about the dispatch of the mission. In a memorandum prepared for President Wilson, Wiseman outlined a series of inter-Allied organs which he thought were needed in order to coordinate the war effort. He named a war council, a joint blockade council, and an economic council.[41] Wiseman wanted House to participate in the establishment of these institutions, but he counseled against sending a permanent mission to Europe similar to those established by the Allies in the United States. He thought the presence of a permanent group in France representing the American government would tend to shift the center of the war effort away from Washington. These comments carried great weight with President Wilson, who wanted to retain the greatest possible control over the development of the American war effort.[42]

The mission finally appointed by President Wilson included representatives from the principal wartime agencies of the American government. Delegates from the Treasury, the War Trade Board, the Shipping Board, the Food Administration, and the War Industries Board joined Colonel House's entourage. Admiral William S. Benson, the Chief of Naval Operations, represented the Navy Department, and General Tasker H. Bliss, the new Chief of Staff, represented the War Department. The members of the mission were sent specifically to consult with their opposite numbers in the Entente governments in order to coordinate the economic and military effort of the United States with that of the Allies.[43] The House mission was instructed to concentrate primarily on the technical aspects of cooperation. Its principal function was to instill much-needed efficiency into inter-Allied activities.[44] Unforeseen circumstances conspired to enlarge the scope of House's activities beyond the original intent.

By late 1917 the best-informed observers were convinced that increased cooperation among the members of the Western coalition was a fundamental condition of victory. The military position of the Allies had deteriorated alarmingly. Sir William Wiseman perhaps summed up the situation most cogently:

> With us [the Allies] there has never been anything like really close cooperation in a political and military sense, and it is probably this more than anything else which has caused so many disappointments to the Allies. When we have attempted at Allied Councils to review the situation broadly and impartially, we find some member putting forth suggestions or objections based on the narrower advantage of his own country rather than of the Cause.[45]

Improved methods of inter-Allied cooperation were definitely needed in order to forestall a great defeat at the hands of the Central Powers during 1918. The extreme seriousness of the military and political situation forced President Wilson to alter his original policy of avoiding detailed political-military consultations with the Entente Powers of Europe.

During November and December 1917 the Allied and Associated Powers established several institutions specifically designed to improve inter-Allied consultation and cooperation. The most important of these was the Supreme War Council. The United States government took an active part in most of these institutions—including the Supreme War Council—but the nature of American cooperation with the Allies had been generally defined before these organizations began to operate.

The United States was already wedded to a political-military outlook which her leaders would not be disposed to alter greatly in substance. The American commitment to a policy which envisioned a postwar society based on a universal dominion of right and to a strategy based on a plan to concentrate an independent American army in France became firmer as time slipped past. The President believed a decisive military triumph over Germany was a necessary prelude to a postwar settlement capable of ordering the future affairs of mankind. In his war message of April 1917 President Wilson had expressed a clear-cut desire to pursue the war cooperatively with the Entente Powers, but the political-military decisions made by the American government in 1917 established limits to such cooperation. American plans reflected a definite disposition to cooperate as fully as possible with the Allies in military operations on the Western Front, but the President plainly intended to avoid political entanglements which he thought might be embarrassing at the time of the postwar peace conference. Only the desperate military and political crises which beset the Western coalition in 1917 caused him to sanction the dispatch of the House mission to Europe for the purpose of improving inter-Allied cooperation.

CHAPTER 2

Establishment of the Supreme War Council

LONG before the United States entered World War I, the Allied Powers had become aware of the weakness resulting from the failure to coordinate their efforts on the Western Front. Unfortunately for the Allies, several early attempts to improve inter-Allied cooperation had come to naught. During 1915-1916 a series of Anglo-French military conferences had been held at General Joffre's headquarters in order to concert strategy, but the results had been highly disappointing. The conferences were significant but insufficient steps in the right direction. The participants had simply prepared military plans for reference to separate political conferences which generally accepted the proposals without discussion. This arrangement nullified political direction.[1]

When David Lloyd George became Prime Minister of Great Britain late in 1916, he inaugurated a new effort to achieve better inter-Allied cooperation. Early in 1917 he succeeded in establishing a joint command of the British and French forces on the Western Front for the purpose of conducting a massive offensive against Germany. General Joffre had been relieved of his authority late in 1916, and General Nivelle, a hero of the battle of Verdun, was elevated to the command of the French army. Lloyd

George was strongly attracted to Nivelle, and he succeeded in arranging his appointment to the supreme command of the projected offensive. Lloyd George's principal military advisors opposed the new command arrangement and the plans concerted at the Calais Conference on 26-27 February 1917, because, among other things, they feared that a French commander might sacrifice control of the strategic Channel ports, upon which the British relied extensively, in favor of the defense of Paris. The Calais Agreement represented an approach to unity of command. Nivelle persuasively advocated a plan based on a quick, huge penetration of the German lines to be followed by a massive pursuit of the fleeing enemy. The action was to be decisive.[2]

The Nivelle Offensive, launched in April 1917, was a tragic failure. The German High Command in France received reinforcements from the east when the initial stage of the Russian Revolution undermined resistance on the Eastern Front. The Germans fortified a new position, the Hindenburg Line, and then conducted a masterful withdrawal to the new fortifications. This movement shortened their front and allowed then to strengthen their defenses. Nivelle then had to postpone his attack. The German army successfully contained an offensive undertaken by the British in the region of Arras as a prelude to the main attack and then concentrated divisions in the Aisne sector to meet the well-advertised French offensive. Both the British and the French suffered huge casualties without making appreciable gains. It was truly a smashing defeat.[3] The Nivelle catastrophe naturally strengthened the arguments of those who opposed a unified command and extensive inter-Allied cooperation. The defeat was frequently recalled whenever unity of command was proposed as a means of increasing the efficiency of the Allied forces in France.

The crushing losses encouraged a wave of widespread

dissatisfaction and even mutiny in many units of the French army. General Pétain replaced Nivelle as commander-in-chief of the French army and eventually managed to restore the shattered morale of his troops. Although Pétain conducted a few limited offensives during the latter months of 1917, the French army remained generally inactive until 1918.[4]

The defeat of the French placed the main burden of operations on the British army for the remainder of 1917. Field Marshal Sir Douglas Haig, the British commander-in-chief, hoped to divert attention from the French, to recapture the Belgian Channel ports from which German submarines were operating so effectively, and to lessen the pressure on Russia. He planned to launch an extensive offensive in Flanders. Although his attack began auspiciously, the British army soon bogged down in the mud around Passchendaele Ridge. There followed several months of excruciating combat with massive losses and meager gains. The morale of the British army did not break as badly as that of the French, but the ranks were exhausted and disheartened. A severe rebuff following a transient success at Cambrai early in November served only to emphasize the degradation of Passchendaele.[5]

Throughout 1917 the German undersea raiders exacted a frightening toll of Allied shipping. These losses seriously interfered with the supply lines of the Entente Powers and the transport of American troops to France. The sea power of Great Britain, reinforced by the United States Navy, set itself to protect merchantmen and destroy submarines. The adoption of the convoy system and the development of new anti-submarine techniques lessened the effectiveness of the German efforts by the end of 1917, but the submarine remained a source of anxiety throughout the rest of the war.[6]

Great as were the disappointments in the west, the defection of Russia in the east was an even more unsettling omen of defeat. The provisional government which had ousted the Czar early in 1917 sought desperately to keep Russia in the war, but all efforts were in vain. The final action of the Russian army, the "Kerensky Offensive," failed miserably in July. Thenceforth the Bolshevik agitation for "peace, land, and bread" rapidly undermined the provisional government. The end of effective Russian resistance enabled the German High Command to contemplate the transfer of many veteran divisions to the Western Front where a powerful concentration was underway, preliminary to a great offensive in 1918.[7]

The final blow of 1917 was the Italian collapse which developed with explosive suddenness late in October. A few German divisions associated with the Austrian army utilized new tactics of surprise to rout the Italian army at Caporetto. With Anglo-French assistance, the Italian generals managed to stabilize their position along the Piave River just north of Venice, but not before absorbing staggering losses.[8]

This long train of disasters, alleviated only by the American entrance into the war, finally brought both the French and the British governments to realize that some form of superior political-military direction was a necessary condition of victory.[9] Several obvious conditions had inhibited effective inter-Allied cooperation before the serious crisis which developed late in 1917. The various Entente Powers espoused differing war aims. Internal civil-military controversies within Britain and France hampered progress. Honest differences of opinion on grand strategy stimulated distrust. Despite these impediments, the need for enhanced coordination could no longer be ignored after the gloomy events of 1917. The creation of the Supreme War Council, specifically founded to achieve inter-Allied coordination, occurred shortly after the Italian defeat at Caporetto, but the negotiations which preceded its formation had begun several months earlier in response to the failure of the great Allied offensives in France and the increasing debility of Russia.[10] The Allied statesman chiefly responsible for the establishment of the Supreme War Council was Prime Minister Lloyd George of Great Britain.

THE ORIGINS OF THE SUPREME WAR COUNCIL, SEPTEMBER-NOVEMBER 1917

Unbowed by adversity, Lloyd George maintained his interest in inter-Allied cooperation as a solution to the difficulties of the Western coalition. Disgusted with the general conduct of the war, he became thoroughly alienated from his principal military counsellors, particularly General Sir William Robertson, the Chief of the Imperial General Staff, and Field Marshal Sir Douglas Haig, the commander-in-chief of the British Expeditionary Forces in France. Both Robertson and Haig were firm supporters of the strategy of concentration on the Western Front, a view Lloyd George found increasingly distasteful. Both soldiers stood high in the affections of the British public. Both had opposed the command of Nivelle which Lloyd George had advocated strenuously. After Nivelle's failure, Lloyd George became a persuasive advocate of "sideshows" in secondary theaters. He believed the logic of events had dictated a pervasive change in inter-Allied planning. To accomplish this task he had to discover some means of coping with Haig and Robertson while retaining the confidence of the nation in arms.[11] Since he had alienated a large group of Liberals, members of his own political party, he had to depend on a doubtful group of Conservatives to sustain his parliamentary majority.

In September 1917 Lloyd George launched a scheme

to bring about a change in strategy without causing the resignations of his recalcitrant soldiers. His first move was to convey his views on strategy and inter-Allied cooperation to the President of the United States.[12] On 3 September he wrote to Wilson propounding his arguments for a new strategy which would eliminate futile frontal attacks on the Western Front. Favoring operations in secondary theaters, he called for the establishment of an institution to coordinate the activities of the Allies:

> I am convinced from my experience of the last three years that the comparative failure of the Allies in 1917 is also in some measure due to defects in their mutual arrangements for conducting the war. . . . There has never been an Allied Body which had knowledge of the resources of all the Allies which could prepare a single coordinated plan for utilizing those resources in the most decisive manner, and at the most decisive points, looking at the front of the Central Powers as a whole and taking into account their political, economic, and diplomatic as well as their military weaknesses. . . . What I have said will be sufficient, I think, to make it clear that if we are to make the best possible use of the forces at the disposal of the Allies, it is of supreme importance to establish effective unity in the direction of the war on the Allied side. . . . In my opinion it will be necessary to establish some kind of Allied Joint Council, with permanent military and probably naval and economic staffs attached to work out the plans for the Allies, for submission to the several Governments concerned.[13]

Lloyd George concluded significantly with a strong plea for active American participation in the determination of inter-Allied plans.

The Prime Minister then proceeded to Paris. On 25 September he discussed his project with Paul Painlevé, the Premier of France, but avoided the issue of sideshows.

The French were particularly interested in achieving unity of command on the Western Front under a French generalissimo, but they favored maintenance of the strategy of concentration in France. They feared that operations of magnitude elsewhere might lead to further German conquest and territorial occupation in their homeland. Painlevé suggested the establishment of an inter-Allied council of war over which General Foch, the French Chief of Staff, would preside. He knew that Lloyd George, faced with opposition at home, could not yet agree to the appointment of a generalissimo, but he hoped the council of war would eventually evolve into a supreme command. After these preliminaries, Painlevé agreed to negotiate the details of the plan at a later date in London.[14]

By this time the futility of Haig's attacks in Flanders near Passchendaele had become apparent. This development strengthened Lloyd George's resolve to circumvent his military counsellors and adopt a new strategy.[15]

The next step was to prepare the British War Cabinet for the scheme. Lloyd George requested Lord French, formerly the British commander-in-chief, and General Sir Henry Wilson, then a favorite of the Prime Minister, to submit reports to him outlining their opinions on strategy for the future. Haig and Robertson also presented memoranda, which merely reiterated their previous views. Haig particularly objected to unity of command and operations in secondary theaters.[16] Both French and Wilson recommended the creation of an inter-Allied body along the lines projected by Lloyd George and Painlevé.[17]

Painlevé arrived in London at the end of October to discuss the inter-Allied war committee. These negotiations clearly revealed the French preference for a generalissimo. Painlevé viewed the proposed committee as a stepping stone to that end. Lloyd George, taking into account the

British fear that a French commander might sacrifice the vital cross-Channel ports to the Germans in favor of the defense of Paris, supported an inter-Allied council rather than a supreme commander with large powers. He believed British public opinion would allow him to proceed no further.[18] The French sought unity of command rather than changes in strategy; Lloyd George coveted a great strategic *démarche* and unity of control by a politically dominated inter-Allied group.

The discussions in London turned on the French desire to assign the several chiefs of staff to the Council, which would sit in Paris. Lloyd George adamantly opposed a grant of power to his enemy, Robertson. One of his principal reasons for advocating the establishment of a council was to circumvent his own military advisors. He wanted the council to sit in Boulogne, one of the vital Channel ports, well removed from the atmosphere of the French capital. These issues were not resolved in London. On 30 October Lloyd George officially proposed the establishment of a "joint council" in a letter to Painlevé. The French agreed in principle to the establishment of an inter-Allied council, and later the British War Cabinet acquiesced.[19]

The battle of Caporetto was just then in its most serious phase, and the two premiers decided to visit their beleaguered Italian associates to concert assistance for the Italian army and to obtain acceptance of the projected council. Lloyd George thought of Caporetto as a final justification for the course he was pursuing.[20] In one sense it was a blessing in disguise; it enabled him to force an early establishment of a political agency to undertake the superior direction of the war.

Before proceeding to Rapallo, the small town in Italy where the Allies planned to meet, Lloyd George asked General Pershing to accompany him. The American commander-in-chief refused, arguing that the purpose of the meeting was overtly political in nature. He later expressed opposition to "war by committee." Consequently no American participated in the founding of the Supreme War Council.[21]

THE RAPALLO CONFERENCE, 7 NOVEMBER 1917

Lloyd George and Painlevé compromised the issues which divided them during the sessions at Rapallo. The British leader circumvented the appointment of chiefs of staff as military advisors of the council, but Painlevé succeeded in locating the institution at Versailles—very near if not in Paris. The Italians accepted the Anglo-French proposal mostly because the first task of the new organization would be to recommend measures for the defense of the Piave front.[22]

The text of the Rapallo Agreement establishing the Supreme War Council follows.

Scheme of Organization of a Supreme War Council

II.(1.) With a view to the better co-ordination of military action on the Western Front a Supreme War Council is created, composed of the Prime Minister and a Member of the Government of each of the Great Powers whose armies are fighting on that front. The extension of the scope of the Council to other fronts is reserved for discussion with the other Great Powers.

(2.) The Supreme War Council has for its mission to watch over the general conduct of the war. It prepares recommendations for the decision of the Governments, and keeps itself informed of their execution and reports thereon to the respective Governments.

(3.) The General Staffs and Military Commands of

each Power charged with the conduct of military operations remain responsible to their respective Governments.

(4.) The general war plans drawn up by the competent Military Authorities are submitted to the Supreme War Council, which, under the high authority of the Governments, ensures their concordance, and submits, if need be, any necessary changes.

(5.) Each Power delegates to the Supreme War Council one Permanent Military Representative whose exclusive function is to act as technical adviser to the Council.

(6.) The Military Representatives receive from the Government and the competent Military Authorities of their country all the proposals, information, and documents relating to the conduct of the war.

(7.) The Military Representatives watch day by day the situation of the forces, and the means of all kinds of which the Allied armies and the enemy armies dispose.

(8.) The Supreme War Council meets normally at Versailles, where the Permanent Military Representatives and their staffs are established. They may meet at other places as may be agreed upon, according to circumstances. The meetings of the Supreme War Council will take place at least once a month.[23]

This Scheme of Organization indicates clearly that Lloyd George gained most of his aims at Rapallo. The Council was made up of political leaders. It received competent military advice from distinguished soldiers who stood outside the regular command and staff echelons of their respective armies. The recommendations of the military representatives were to have great weight, but the representatives did not sit on the Council itself. The Council was an advisory organ designed to concert various recommendations which its members would implement by coordinated action. Its mission was defined broadly, but its membership excluded Russia and lesser Allies like Belgium.

The provision for regular sessions was one of its most unusual features. By separating the functions of the military representatives from those of the national military establishments, the Council became a coordinating agency standing above the individual general staffs. It invoked the sanction of the several governments as its authority.

The Supreme War Council was a compromise. Although it failed to meet French aspirations for a supreme command, it constituted a significant reaction against the lack of coordination which had frustrated inter-Allied efforts on the Western Front. By establishing political control of military operations, it was in accord with the principle of civilian predominance over the military. Its organization was an implicit rejection of the narrow nationalism which had so obviously impeded inter-Allied cooperation. It was to become a clearing house for differences in national points of view and an environment in which disagreements could be exposed and often resolved in the interest of victory.

THE HOUSE MISSION IN EUROPE

The House Mission, sent to Europe by President Wilson specifically to assist in the process of coordinating inter-Allied efforts against the Central Powers, landed in Great Britain on the day the Rapallo Agreement was signed by the Entente leaders. From this time on the United States became more and more closely associated with inter-Allied planning. The period of relative abstention from European conferences was at an end. Henceforth the history of American policy and strategy during World War I becomes inextricably intertwined with the history of inter-Allied cooperation.

As soon as the Mission arrived in London, its members

began extended consultations with their counterparts in the British government. The general conference in Paris was postponed due to the uncertainties created by the Bolshevik assumption of power in Russia and by the parliamentary crises in both Britain and France when the creation of the Supreme War Council was announced.[24]

Despite speeches in Paris by Lloyd George and Painlevé designed to garner support for the Council, the French government fell on 13 November.[25] The vote of no confidence came on a relatively minor issue; just previously the Assembly had voted to sustain the decision to establish the Supreme War Council. Nevertheless, Painlevé's failure to obtain the appointment of a French generalissimo contributed to the irritations which led to his overthrow.[26]

Lloyd George also had to cope with a political crisis directly related to the establishment of the Council. Realizing that his ministry was in danger, he sought American indorsement of the Rapallo Agreement in order to undermine his Parliamentary critics.[27] House refused to concur until he had received instructions, but his recommendation to President Wilson proposed a qualified acceptance. He suggested that General Bliss be appointed the American military representative but advised against seating a political delegate. "It is necessary," he concluded, "to encourage our friends here and in France."[28] This observation reflected his awareness that Entente morale had been seriously damaged by the crushing disasters of 1917. Nevertheless House's early attempt to eliminate American *political* representation in the Council reflects the strong American opposition to joint diplomatic cooperation.

The President responded immediately, indorsing the scheme and authorizing the appointment of General Bliss. "Please take the position," he told House, "that we not only approve a continuance of the plan for a war council but insist on it."[29] House then issued a paraphrase of the President's message which simply supported "unity of control between all the Allies and the United States" without specifically approving the Rapallo Agreement. He hoped to avoid a charge that he had interfered in a domestic political dispute. After a momentary period of uncertainty and an acrimonious debate in the Commons, Lloyd George managed to retain his place.[30] House obtained the Prime Minister's consent to a session of the Supreme War Council in conjunction with the inter-Allied conference in Paris. The President had asked him to attend at least one meeting before returning to the United States.[31]

The Colonel definitely disliked the important role in the Council assigned to politicians, but his willingness to seat General Bliss as military representative demonstrated his interest in achieving military unity of plan and control. In accordance with the President's policy, House sought to avoid diplomatic entanglements which might prejudice the American plans for the peace settlement. House knew of the struggle between Lloyd George and Robertson. The Parliamentary debate had turned on this issue, and the Prime Minister had strongly repudiated the French plan to create a supreme commander at some future time. His stand naturally was ill received in Paris. By emphasizing the advisory nature of the Supreme War Council, Lloyd George somewhat weakened its prestige.[32]

After considering the plan drafted at Rapallo, House and Bliss began to evolve a revision to insure that the Council would strengthen inter-Allied unity of plan and control without stimulating international disputes of a political nature. The House Mission departed for Paris on 22 November. Once in the French capital, House and Bliss seized the opportunity to explore the subject of the Council with the new French Premier, Georges Clemenceau.

Clemenceau seemed quite responsive to the American arguments in favor of revising the Rapallo Agreement. House then reported to the President:

> The French want a "Generalissimo" but they want him to be a Frenchman. This . . . would meet with so much opposition in England that it is not to be thought of. Any Government that proposed it would be overthrown. . . . [Clemenceau] is earnestly in favor of unity of plan and action, but he thinks as I do that the plan of Lloyd George is not workable, and for reasons somewhat similar to those I have given. . . . He wants us to take the initiative and he promises that we can count upon him to back to a finish any reasonable suggestion that we make.[33]

Encouraged by the French reaction, General Bliss drew up a draft proposal entitled "Unity of Control" which envisioned a "purely military council" made up of the commanders-in-chief of the national armies together with the several chiefs of staff. Bliss also called for the appointment of a "President" who would be elected by the members and would have the power to execute decisions of the panel.[34] This provision was a clear acceptance of the French emphasis on a strong military authority. House and Bliss discussed this plan with Clemenceau and Pétain, both of whom supported it. The French specifically supported the elimination of political representatives from the Supreme War Council, the aspect of the Rapallo Agreement so important to Lloyd George.[35]

The British leader utterly refused to accept the revision, threatening to leave Paris if his plan were jettisoned.[36] His action forced House and Bliss to suspend their conversations, and the Rapallo Agreement remained unchanged. Colonel House, highly irritated by this setback, was inclined to dismiss the Council as of small utility due to the intransigence of Lloyd George.[37] Obviously the latter could not accept the muscular proposals of Bliss, which smacked distinctly of a supreme command and which also left power in the hands of Haig and Robertson. House and Bliss mistakenly thought the Council would normally originate military plans as well as coordinate inter-Allied activity. This misapprehension was later dispelled when the Council's functions had been defined by experience. This early disposition to discount the importance of the Supreme War Council definitely colored the American attitude toward it for some time to come.[38]

The general inter-Allied conference in Paris functioned quite effectively. The American military and naval plans were discussed extensively with the Entente leaders, and detailed recommendations emanated from the sessions. In addition, significant steps were taken to coordinate finance, shipping, blockade policy, and materials. The conference confined itself to these subjects, generally avoiding consideration of higher policy.[39]

While in Paris, Colonel House decided to press the Entente for a general inter-Allied statement of war aims. This attempt failed completely despite a considerable effort by the Colonel.[40] The new rulers of Russia, the Bolshevik revolutionaries, were pressing for a pronouncement of war aims, and Colonel House believed a response to this agitation might possibly keep Russia in the war.[41] He did not expect the Allies to discuss or publicize their detailed territorial aims.[42] President Wilson approved House's design, strongly deprecating "selfish aims." The American people, he thought, would refuse to fight for them. "I think," he concluded somewhat ominously, "it will be obvious to all that it would be a fatal mistake to cool the ardor in America."[43] These events constituted a prelude to the President's enunciation of the Fourteen Points in January 1918.

THE SECOND SESSION OF THE SUPREME WAR COUNCIL

The culminating event of the Colonel's stay in Paris was the Second Session of the Supreme War Council held on 1 December at Versailles. Clemenceau began the meeting with a general statement of the Council's immediate problems. In his view its first tasks were to consider the plan of campaign for 1918, the repercussions of the Russian defection, military assistance for Italy, the nature of American activity in 1918, and the military situation in the Balkans.[44] Under pressure from Lloyd George, he posed the issue of campaigns in secondary theaters. He emphasized that the military representatives would offer independent advice to the whole Council. They would not function as advocates of national desires.[45] After a series of resolutions were passed which dealt with the organization and procedure of the Council, the Session ended with what Colonel House considered "rather desultory conversation." The American delegate and General Bliss took little part in the debates, believing that they should withhold opinions on military subjects until the American army appeared in force on the Western Front. Then, wrote House to the President, "it will be another story."[46]

Disturbed that nothing more concrete had been decided, House confided his irritation to his diary. "Nothing is buttoned up with the Allies; it is all talk and no concerted action."[47] He felt the Supreme War Council should have "formulated policy . . . as broad, as far-reaching, and as effective as the coordination of our military, naval, and economic resources [has] been." [48] In this mood the Colonel returned to the United States.

The final reports of the members of the House Mission uniformly stressed the seriousness of the situation and the immense need for inter-Allied cooperation.[49]

General Bliss reacted strongly to the lack of coordination exhibited by the Entente Powers. Pointing out that a great military crisis impended in the spring of 1918, he particularly deprecated the inability of the Allies to concert their strategy:

> This crisis is largely due to the collapse of Russia as a military factor and to the recent crisis in Italy. But it is also largely due to the lack of military coordination, lack of unity of control on the part of the allied forces in the field.
>
> This lack of unity results from military jealousy and suspicion as to ultimate national aims.[50]

Bliss suggested that the United States make its reinforcements contingent upon European acceptance of unity of control, "even going if necessary (and I believe it is) to the limit of unified command." He thought the military men of Europe would welcome unity of control if political meddling were not involved. After castigating the politicians for failing to grasp the necessity of unity, he concluded that they might now be amenable to "intelligent pressure."

Colonel House's report also dwelt on the lack of inter-Allied unity. "If this war is to be won, better team work between the Allies must be effected. . . . Unless a change for the better comes the Allies cannot win, and Germany may." He included a significant comment on the Supreme War Council:

> The Supreme War Council as presently constituted is almost a farce. It could be the efficient instrument to win the war. The United States can make it so, and I hope she will exercise her undisputed power to do it.[51]

The establishment of the Supreme War Council late in 1917 was an attempt to coordinate the war effort of the

Allied and Associated Powers in the face of a great crisis. Even in the depths of the emergency, there were numerous indications that the American government would strenuously oppose inter-Allied projects of a political-military nature which might unduly prejudice the fundamental war aims and postwar plans of the United States. Nevertheless, the American preoccupation with increased military and economic cooperation reflected a strong desire to achieve a decisive victory over the Central Powers. The House-Bliss effort to eliminate political representation on the Supreme War Council clearly indicated their desire to utilize the Council primarily to obtain military unity of plan and control. Already the American relation to the Council had been greatly influenced by the national desire to impose upon the belligerents of both armed camps a farsighted and magnanimous peace. President Wilson, hitherto concerned mostly with the massive task of internal organization for war, would now begin to consider more deeply the broader political-military problems which Colonel House had encountered during his visit to Europe.

CHAPTER 3

Institutional Characteristics of the Supreme War Council

THE Supreme War Council was pre-eminently a political organization designed to concert inter-Allied strategy. Since it brought together the most important political and military leaders of the Allied and Associated Powers, it provided an unusual opportunity to resolve issues which required joint consultation.[1] Hastily organized and hurriedly put to work, the Council developed its procedures under the impact of the great events of 1918. It was a unique institution designed to cope with the unprecedented problems of cooperation which challenged the Western coalition during the decisive phase of the war.[2]

THE FUNCTIONS OF THE SUPREME WAR COUNCIL

The Council met eight times during the last year of the war at intervals of approximately a month.[3] Only heads of government or their deputies and one other representative from each country sat on the Council, although the military representatives and other important soldiers and statesmen often attended and participated in debate.[4] Ordinarily Prime Minister Lloyd George and Secretary of State for War Lord Milner represented Britain. Premier Clemenceau and Foreign Minister Stephen Pichon sat for France.

Premier Vittorio Orlando and Foreign Minister Sydney Sonnino appeared for Italy. President Wilson was the official American delegate, but he never attended. Colonel House represented him at the second session in December 1917 and the eighth session late in October 1918. At the other sessions the United States did not seat a political delegate. Spokesmen for the lesser Allies attended only when business directly affecting them was under discussion. Since most of the meetings took place at Versailles, Clemenceau, the host premier, normally served as presiding officer.[5]

The Council was not an executive agency, its principal function being to prepare joint recommendations on grand strategy, which were referred to the various governments for their acceptance, rejection, or modification. The recommendations were not approved until each of the four nations represented on the Council had given its consent. The plans of the Council were implemented by coordinated inter-Allied action. The agenda of the organization provided for discussion of joint notes prepared by the military representatives. No joint note was submitted to the Council for consideration unless it had been unanimously accepted by the military representatives. The provision for unanimity tended to exert pressure for compromise as well as to eliminate obviously irreconcilable issues. Bliss drew attention to this tendency:

> Every military plan made here is necessarily a compromise. If one of the [Military Representatives] knows that his Government will not approve he refuses to give his assent. But if we believe that the Allies in general desire us to accept a plan each of us surrenders such of his objections as are not radical in order to reach an agreement and we leave to the respective governments to dictate modifications of it. Otherwise any action here would be impossible.[6]

The formal sessions of the Council officially considered and approved decisions which usually had been reached previously by means of informal discussions held in conjunction with the official gathering. General Bliss explained this aspect of the Council's procedure to Colonel House when he came to Paris for the pre-armistice discussions in October 1918:

> Before a session of the War Council, the three Prime Ministers have agreed as far as they can agree, on the important questions that are to come up. . . . You can see that, as a result of this, the proceedings are "cut-and-dried." The meeting does no more than record the agreement already reached. I told Mr. House that in my opinion he cannot conduct important business in the open sessions of the War Council; that his real business must be transacted individually with the Prime Ministers, to whom he may have occasion to say many things he would not want to say in an open session of the War Council.[7]

Thus much of the history of the Supreme War Council centers on the private consultations which transpired prior to the official debates.

The joint notes drawn up by the military representatives dealt with broad military questions which could be decided only by heads of government. Although these recommendations often were expressed in detail, they ordinarily did not impinge on the prerogatives of field commanders. They established the limits within which commanders were to conduct their operations.[8] This practice imparted a speed and efficiency which had been signally absent during the earlier phases of the war.[9]

To provide technical advice on special subjects, the Supreme War Council developed several auxiliary committees which proved quite useful. Among these were committees on tanks, aviation, naval liaison, and anti-aircraft. Their membership was drawn from the staffs of the military representatives.[10]

There were, of course, several other inter-Allied organs not directly affiliated with the Supreme War Council. Among these were the Allied Naval Council, the Inter-Allied [land] Transportation Council, the Allied Blockade Council, the Allied Food Council, the Allied Munitions Council, and the Allied Council on War Purchases and Finance. The Supreme War Council had dealings with most of these institutions. Since the Versailles group was the only inter-Allied body on which the prime ministers themselves sat, it functioned on occasion as a clearing house for recommendations from other coordinating agencies.[11]

Certain military recommendations required joint consultation with members of the Allied Naval Council. Admiral William S. Sims, the commander of American naval forces in European waters, represented the United States on that body. Several joint meetings were held in 1918, the most important being a discussion of armistice terms in October. In general, the joint consultations were of slight significance.[12]

General Bliss never tired of emphasizing that a great coalition required "unity of national purposes, fully supported by each national will." The function of the Supreme War Council was to concert that unity.[13]

THE FUNCTIONS OF THE PERMANENT MILITARY REPRESENTATIVES

The permanent military representatives were supposed to be independent counsellors responsible to the whole Council rather than to their respective governments.[14] Lloyd George specifically designed the board of military representatives to exclude chiefs of staff and commanders-in-chief. For this reason, General Foch, the chief of staff of the French army who had been named the first military representative of France, was replaced by his right-hand man, General Maxime Weygand.[15] General Bliss retired as the American chief of staff before taking his place at Versailles.[16]

The function of the military representatives envisioned by Lloyd George did not survive the early experience of the group at Versailles. The appointment of Weygand insured close relations between Foch and the French Section. After General Sir Henry Wilson, the first British military representative, became chief of the Imperial General Staff in succession to Robertson, his successors, particularly General C. G. Sackville-West, cooperated closely with the British General Staff. General Bliss deferred punctiliously to both General Pershing in France and the War Department in Washington. The Italians, never very active at Versailles, customarily remained in the background. Consequently the military representatives ordinarily presented the views of their respective countries, but the close associations which developed at Versailles did much to minimize controversies between the various Sections.[17]

The principal occupation of the military representatives was to prepare joint notes for presentation to the Supreme War Council. For this purpose they met regularly, a total of fifty-one times from 4 December 1917 to 11 November 1918.[18] They discussed given subjects in response to requests from their particular governments, the Supreme War Council, or individual representatives. Seeking to avoid undue controversies, the group did not forward joint notes to the Supreme War Council unless they were unanimously approved by themselves.[19]

The joint notes normally referred only to the military aspects of the situation at hand. Political problems were discussed through diplomatic channels or at the formal sessions of the Supreme War Council. After the original proposal had been drafted in one of the Sections and distributed to the others, informal discussions ensued which gave the draft note's proponents a chance to estimate the prospect of its adoption. This process often led to revision or rejection of the proposal. The notes contained three parts: the authorization or reason for presentation, the factors taken into consideration, and the conclusions or recommendations.[20] The representatives studiously avoided public disagreements and maintained excellent personal relationships, although inevitable professional differences developed on occasion.[21]

In order to facilitate exchange of information between the Sections, a Joint Secretariat was established, the American member being Colonel U. S. Grant III. The Secretariat arranged agenda for meetings of both the Supreme War Council and the military representatives. It published the texts and translations of official documents and transmitted them to the several governments.[22]

The board of military representatives performed quite efficiently. If it did not evolve along the lines envisioned at the time of the Rapallo Conference, it eventually developed a smooth-working procedure which did much to enhance the prestige and performance of the Supreme War Council.

THE AMERICAN SECTION AT VERSAILLES

The American Section of the Supreme War Council occupied offices at the Trianon Hotel in Versailles late in January 1918. It was the last of the Sections to begin operations, the others having been at work since early December 1917. The American Section included twelve officers and about forty enlisted men and army field clerks.[23]

General Bliss chose to model his organization after that of the British, the largest and most carefully planned of the other groups. General Sir Henry Wilson had set up five "Branches," each with specific missions. The "A" Branch (Allies) studied the military situation of friendly forces, and the "E" Branch (Enemies) performed the same function for the forces of the Central Powers. Both took into consideration the positions of neutral countries. An "M" Branch (Material and Manpower) dealt with logistical problems, and a "P" Branch (Politics) considered the political conditions which affected military plans. A Secretariat and Administrative Branch disposed of housekeeping.

The American Section consisted of three committees, on Allies, Enemies, and Materials and Manpower, along with a Secretariat. No political committee was created, a decision in accord with the American predisposition to avoid diplomatic entanglements at Versailles.[24] Liaison officers represented General Bliss at General Pershing's headquarters and at General Foch's headquarters after the latter's appointment as commander-in-chief of the Allied forces in France. These officers kept the Section informed of developments at the front.[25]

General Bliss was a seasoned officer with a colorful record that included a goodly amount of political-military experience. He had been the American military attaché in Spain when the Spanish-American War broke out. During that conflict he participated in the invasion of Puerto Rico, and after its conclusion he served as collector of customs during the American occupation of Cuba. He then spent several years in the military government of the Philippines before returning to Washington for a long tour of duty on the General Staff. Bliss was a classical scholar of surprising erudition and a skilled linguist. A reflective man, inclined to contemplation and reading, he possessed personal qualities that endeared him to his associates and particularly qualified him for duty at Versailles.[26] He was perhaps the best-liked and most respected American of high rank who went to Europe during World War I with the possible exception of Colonel House.[27] Since Bliss was the only military representative to retain his position throughout the war, his tenure enhanced his prestige. He continually acted as an intermediary between his colleagues and habitually reconciled disputes.[28]

General Bliss forwarded the texts of joint notes and the transcripts of proceedings at Versailles to the State Department. He did not receive instructions from the Secretary of State and was not directly informed of the State Department's position on foreign policy. Arthur Hugh Frazier, who became counsellor of the American Embassy in Paris during the summer of 1918, was named to assist Bliss as a diplomatic liaison officer. Frazier made direct reports to the State Department.[29] He provided Bliss with political information gleaned at the Embassy. The desire to avoid diplomatic involvements in Europe and the relatively restricted functions of the State Department during President Wilson's administration explain the unimportance of Bliss' ties with the State Department.

The American Section maintained close contact with the War Department. Bliss corresponded regularly with his successor as chief of staff, General Peyton C. March, and with Secretary Baker. In these more or less official communications he reported his activities at great length. His instructions often were conveyed with remarkable informality by Secretary Baker in the form of personal letters. Bliss' letters to Baker and March sometimes were forwarded to the President, who kept them on file.[30]

The American Section had limited dealings with the American Expeditionary Forces. Bliss maintained a liaison officer at Chaumont, Pershing's G.H.Q., but the Section did not provide important services to Pershing's command. Bliss consulted Pershing quite regularly and always deferred to the Commander-in-Chief, even when his judgment differed in important respects. Pershing had sought to have one of his subordinates, General Hunter Liggett, appointed to Versailles. He appears to have been suspicious of General Bliss. The latter's tact seems to have triumphed over Pershing's fears, and the two generals managed to avoid a public quarrel.[31]

The records of the American Section reflect the industry and determination with which the small group pursued their duties. Sometimes disparaged by Pershing's staff, the Section contributed materially to the American effort although overshadowed by the fighting forces.

AMERICA'S AVOIDANCE OF POLITICAL REPRESENTATION AT VERSAILLES

The United States sustained its policy of avoiding political representation on the Supreme War Council until the armistice negotiations took place in October-November 1918. Fearful that American peace plans would be compromised, the President continued to insist on military cooperation without sacrificing his diplomatic independence. Arthur Hugh Frazier monitored meetings of the Supreme War Council but never participated in debates.[32]

Although unwilling to discuss war aims with the Entente Powers, President Wilson reversed his policy of silence by his unilateral announcement of the Fourteen Points on 8 January 1918.[33] In his speech to the Congress he clearly indicated that American aims were not fully in accord with those of the Allies. By emphasizing his desire to negotiate a just peace conditional on the destruction of German militarism, the President forged a propaganda weapon of singular potency.

President Wilson believed the time had come to make some response to the Russian pressure for peace without annexations or indemnities. The time seemed opportune to differentiate American policy from that of the Entente. Colonel House urged this tactic and helped draft the speech with the aid of materials supplied by the Inquiry.[34] Because the American reinforcement had become so important to the Allies, the President felt able to express his views without fear of serious repercussions. The first five points were general statements of principle regarding fundamental aspects of international relations. Wilson called for open covenants openly arrived at, absolute freedom of the seas, establishment of equal conditions of international trade, disarmament, and an equitable adjustment of colonial claims. The next eight points dealt with territorial adjustments and restoration of conquered territory in connection with Russia, Belgium, France, Italy, Austria-Hungary, the Balkans, Turkey, and Poland. The fourteenth point called for a league of nations to guarantee political independence and territorial integrity.[35] Although the Fourteen Points were somewhat vaguely phrased and susceptible of diverse interpretations, they were far more detailed and comprehensive than previous pronouncements. The American government had revised its approach to the peace settlement; henceforth President Wilson spoke unilaterally on war aims, refusing to discuss them with the Allies.

The President's new approach to the peace settlement naturally influenced American contacts with the Entente Powers at inter-Allied gatherings. The Supreme War Council held its first important session at the end of January

1918. Since the topics on the agenda were of great significance, General Bliss sought diplomatic support. He recommended to Washington that the American ambassadors to Britain and France be designated to sit on the Council. "The American military representative," he wrote, "is constantly embarrassed by not having the same political support that the military representatives of the other Allies have." [36] This request was ignored in Washington, and Bliss was left to his own devices. American leaders had determined to pursue a cooperative but independent course.

Any chance that the United States might seat a political delegate at Versailles went glimmering when the Supreme War Council issued a bellicose denunication of the Central Powers at the conclusion of their third session on 4 February 1918.[37] A reference in the document to an "unscrupulous and brutal attempt at domination" contrasted blatantly with the moderate accents of President Wilson's public statements. Colonel House wrote angrily to the President, noting the Council's action and deprecating its possible effect:

> I am disturbed at the statement given out by the civil end of the Supreme War Council. It seems to me a monumental blunder. It is the old belligerent tone and will serve the purpose of again welding together the people of the Central Powers.[38]

Two days later he commented further:

> It is not altogether a bad thing not having a civil representative on the Supreme War Council. If I had been there this statement would not have been issued. Nevertheless, it would have been difficult to keep them from doing something of a similar nature. They tried this repeatedly when I was in Paris, and my mere statement that the United States would not join them, and my cordial advice to go ahead alone, always had the desired effect.[39]

President Wilson continued to hope for a negotiated peace in the spirit of his prewar negotiations with the belligerents, but he believed a decisive military victory was prerequisite to this purpose. American leaders couched their public statements in terms designed to undermine the fighting will of the Central Powers. By adopting a moderate tone in comments about the Central Powers the President hoped to appeal over the heads of their leaders directly to the people in behalf of a benevolent peace settlement.

The President indicated his irritation with the Supreme War Council by ordering Frazier to announce that the United States wished to dissociate itself from political statements of the Council unless the text had previously been approved by himself.[40] He wanted to contradict the inference that the Supreme War Council was competent to express American policy on war aims, a conclusion that easily could have been drawn from the phraseology and presentation of the declaration.

Shortly thereafter a similar act by another inter-Allied organ further alienated the President. The Inter-Allied Council on War Purchases and Finance issued a statement concerning Russia which conveyed distinct political overtones strongly at variance with American policy. Thereupon the President, through Secretary of State Robert Lansing, delivered a strong protest to the ambassadors of the Entente Powers for transmission to their governments:

> I beg to inform you that the President wishes very respectfully to earnestly urge that when he suggested the creation of the Supreme War Council, it was not at all in his mind that [the Supreme War Council and the Inter-Allied Council on War Purchases and Finance] should take any action or express any opinion on political subjects. He would have doubted the wisdom of appointing representatives of this Government had he thought they would undertake the decision of any questions but the very practical

> question of supplies and of the concerted conduct of the war which it was understood they would handle.
>
> He would appreciate it very much if this matter were very thoroughly considered by the political leaders of the governments addressed, and that he might be given an opportunity, should their view in this matter differ from his, to consider once more the conditions and construction under which the representatives of the United States should henceforth act.[41]

Thus the President reasserted his determination to avoid political entanglements that might stem from the activities of inter-Allied organs and defined his conception of the Supreme War Council. This experience clearly strengthened the President's prejudice against the Council.

Throughout his tenure at Versailles, General Bliss felt embarrassed by the President's antipathy toward political representation on the Supreme War Council. The General's position was particularly delicate, because the issues coming before him almost always involved important political questions with which he was not authorized to deal.[42] Bliss was acutely aware of this fact. Occasionally he requested confidential information on American policy which he needed in order to discuss certain issues with his colleagues.[43] Although Secretary of War Baker sometimes passed along hints of American policy, Bliss was never adequately informed. He was constantly handicapped by the American predilection to eschew the political activities of the Council; but, given the President's desire to sustain diplomatic independence, no other course was feasible.

Political participation in the deliberations of the Supreme War Council necessarily would have required a certain amount of compromise, a consequence the President was not prepared to countenance. Bliss succeeded in avoiding political discussions and in lessening the impact of political controversies on military strategy when to do otherwise would have led to disastrous results from the American point of view. His anomalous position long remained a source of insecurity. Fortunately the Allies generally avoided further political statements through the Supreme War Council to which the United States might object.

The President's irritation with the Allies strengthened his determination to make additional comments on war aims. This was done in a message to Congress on 11 February, which included the "Four Principles." The German and Austrian reactions to the Fourteen Points seemed to call for a response which would clarify the moderate position of the United States. The Four Principles constituted a minimal foundation for peace negotiations. The President held that (1) a successful peace settlement would have to be based on the justice of particular cases and their potential for insuring a permanent settlement; (2) peoples and provinces could not be bartered or treated as chattels; (3) territorial settlements would have to be made to accord with the interests of the people directly concerned, rather than to insure a satisfactory compromise between more powerful nations; (4) national aspirations would have to be recognized if they did not introduce undue elements of international discord.[44] Although somewhat vague, the Four Principles represented an important amplification of American war aims. They emphasized the unique purposes of the United States which the President hoped to further by avoiding inter-Allied discussions of war aims.

Shortly thereafter, Hindenburg and Ludendorff launched a powerful German offensive in March 1918, and the President seemed to repudiate his moderate policy in favor of a Carthaginian settlement. Speaking once again to the Congress, he called for "Force, Force to the utmost,

Force without stint or limit, the righteous and triumphant force which shall make Right the law of the world, and cast every selfish dominion down in the dust." [45] His obvious intent was to strengthen the morale of the Allies, then shaken by the most severe military crisis of the war. For the moment, President Wilson appeared to turn his back on a magnanimous peace settlement, but these aspirations would reappear when Germany at last was cast down in the dust. They account in great part for the American refusal to utilize the inevitably restrictive environment of Versailles for important inter-Allied political consultations.

The Supreme War Council was a clearing house for inter-Allied coordination of both strategy and policy. President Wilson, however, refused to permit American participation in its political undertakings. Well aware that his plans for the peace settlement were at some variance with those of the Entente Powers, he sought to avoid political-military involvements which might jeopardize his program. He preferred to wait for the day when American power and prestige would enable him, if necessary, to force acceptance of his desires. He welcomed cooperative military strategy not in conflict with American aspirations which the Supreme War Council could concert, but he was unwilling to move beyond this concession. The historic American distrust of Europe had found expression even in the policy of the man who was incomparably the greatest exponent of international trust and good will in his time.

CHAPTER 4

Evolution of the Unified Command

THE Supreme War Council was created to establish inter-Allied "unity of plan and control." Lloyd George believed the British public would not accept "unity of command," a more advanced technique. Painlevé concurred—with the tacit understanding that in time a Frenchman would be appointed to command the entire Western Front.[1]

Unencumbered by adverse public opinion, the American government had supported a unified command in order to coordinate the Allied effort in France. The American strategy of concentration on the Western Front presupposed military collaboration with France, Italy, and Britain—if that policy did not lead to embarrassing political commitments which might compromise the war aims of the President.

Prior to March 1918 the Supreme War Council attempted to make command arrangements designed to enhance the efficiency of inter-Allied operations on the Western Front and elsewhere. A powerful German offensive in March finally forced the Allied and Associated Powers to a fundamental decision on unity of command. This decision was largely shaped by the Supreme War Council.

STRATEGY FOR 1918 AND THE GENERAL RESERVE

The second session of the Supreme War Council had delegated several important tasks to the permanent military representatives, including the thorny problem of proposing grand strategy for 1918.[2] General Bliss had not yet taken his place at Versailles, but the representatives of Britain, France, and Italy—Generals Sir Henry Wilson, Maxime Weygand, and Luigi Cadorna—almost immediately produced Joint Note No. 1 on "Military Policy." It proposed a defensive strategy in all theaters for 1918 in order to gain time until sufficient American reinforcements arrived in France to warrant a return to the offensive.[3] In January the group developed a detailed proposal, Joint Note No. 12, entitled "1918 Campaign." Although these notes reflected a determination to achieve unity of plan, they did not provide adequate command arrangements.

Joint Note No. 12 combined a qualified optimism with belief that victory could not be gained in 1918. Noting that Britain was safe from assault during the approaching campaign, it held that France and Italy could be defended if American troops arrived in Europe at the rate of two divisions per month. If logistical problems were overcome, "the enemy cannot in 1918 gain a definite military decision in the main theatres which would enable him to break finally the resistance of any of the Allied Powers." Conversely the Allies could not anticipate a favorable decision in France. What could be done in 1918? After noting conditions in the secondary theaters, the military representatives proposed "annihilation" of the Turkish army.[4]

The hand of Lloyd George is quite noticeable in this document. Disillusioned by the failure of frontal attacks in France, the Prime Minister through his associate, General Wilson, pressed for an extensive "sideshow" in order to weaken Germany by destroying one of her lesser partners. The French wished to fight a holding action on the Western Front until enough American troops had arrived to turn the tide. Joint Note No. 12 effected a compromise between these desires.[5]

When the third session of the Supreme War Council met late in January, it approved Joint Note No. 12, but Lloyd George had to accept a proviso designed to prevent a diversion of men and materials to the Middle East if they were needed on the Western Front. A solid phalanx of French leaders, supported by Robertson, Haig, and Pershing, argued that a military adventure in a secondary theater would dangerously undermine the Allied position in France.[6] Lloyd George was unable to implement his plan to "roll up" Turkey, and General Allenby had to continue his brilliant campaign in Palestine without the benefit of the significant reinforcements envisioned by General Wilson. The proposal to knock Turkey out of the war gave notice that Lloyd George did not intend to relax his advocacy of the "eastern strategy" even if it were opposed by almost every important general in his entourage except Wilson. The heated discussion of Joint Note No. 12 exposed the lack of unity which still prevailed in Allied councils.

The military representatives had prepared another project to alleviate the dangers of divided command in France—the "Interallied General Reserve." The General Reserve was designed to provide a defensive counterpoise to the German offensive expected to begin about the middle of April in France. The French leaders warmly supported the General Reserve, which promised greater security on the Western Front. Foch and Wilson drew up the initial plan and explained it to the principal Allied generals at Compiègne on 24 January 1918. The Wilson-Foch proposal contemplated an inter-Allied maneuver force of some thirty divisions based on several strategic points behind the front. From these locations the Reserve could move promptly to the support of any portion of the front which might receive a strong German attack. Foch wanted to hold part of the force as a counterattacking element in order to take advantage of any weak spots in the German line. The French still wished to establish a unified command, but they supported the General Reserve because it seemed to be the only plan the British would accept.

Both Haig and Pétain, the commanders-in-chief of the British and French armies, vigorously criticized the plan for the General Reserve. General Robertson suggested that Haig and Pétain be commissioned to draw up plans for mutual support, should the Germans attack either the British or the French strongly enough to require reinforcements from the other.[7] The reaction against the General Reserve reflected the military jealousies both within and between countries which disturbed inter-Allied relationships. It also pinpointed the specific British distrust of movements in the direction of a unified command.

Choosing to ignore Robertson's plan, the military representatives decided to present Note No. 14 on the "General Reserve" to the approaching session of the Supreme War Council.[8] They avoided the subject of who would command the General Reserve. General Weygand argued that the force could not function without a commander-in-chief, but General Wilson refused to condone such an appointment.[9] The note merely proposed a General Reserve, leaving to the Supreme War Council to rule on the knotty problems of composition and command.

At this opportune juncture General Bliss arrived at Versailles. Reflecting the views of the American General Staff, he was a convinced supporter of unity of plan and control and more particularly of unified command. After the battle of Caporetto the Army War College had composed a memorandum for General Bliss, putting the case for unity of command in the strongest terms:

> The sole direction is obligatory in battle. . . . It is no less necessary in the general conduct, political and military, of the war. . . . The longer the Allies put off this unanimity of direction the more they run risks capable of compromising the ultimate success. . . . We conclude that the Allies are unable to win unless they make certain from the beginning of an *administration of the war* extending to all human activities bent toward the war. . . . The multiplicity of fronts and of interest, the complications of operation [make] necessary an administrative body possessing more extensive power than a military conference and above all a *permanent* body.[10]

Composed a month before the formation of the Supreme War Council and six months before the establishment of Foch's supreme command, this memorandum reveals the American belief that problems of cooperation constituted a most formidable obstacle to ultimate victory.[11]

General Bliss wanted his government to take the lead in the campaign to establish a unified command. He pressed the matter forcibly in a message to Secretary Baker:

> The United States is now in a position to take the lead in bringing about absolute unity of control in this matter [the General Reserve] and probably in the others which are vital to our success in the prosecution of the war. Unless the United States takes such action I doubt whether unity of control over any of these things will be secured.[12]

The plan for the General Reserve bore marked similarities to the House-Bliss proposal for the reform of the Supreme War Council which had been rejected during the Paris conference. Bliss became an ardent supporter of the General Reserve.

When the Supreme War Council met on 30 January 1918, Haig, Pétain, and Robertson argued cogently against the General Reserve, maintaining that the Allies lacked the manpower to implement it and that an arrangement between the French and British armies would cover the situation. Bliss boldly called for the appointment of a commander for the General Reserve, but the British vetoed this plan.[13]

After further haggling, the Council decided to constitute an "Executive War Board" composed of the military representatives of Britain, Italy, and the United States, with General Foch for France. This body was to plan and administer the General Reserve. It would be headed by a "president," who would obviously be General Foch. The final draft of the resolution passed by the Council establishing the Reserve was a modification of the proposal put forth by General Bliss at the Paris conference in November 1917.[14]

The Executive War Board was empowered to prepare the General Reserve and to determine the direction of its movements. Once the Reserve had been committed, its command would revert to the field headquarters receiving the troops. A proviso was incorporated into the resolution to protect national interests against unacceptable actions by the Executive War Board: "In case of irreconcilable differences of opinion on a point of importance connected with the General Reserve, any Military Representative has the right to appeal to the Supreme War Council." The approval of the General Reserve was a distinct turning point in inter-Allied relationships. Bliss noted its importance later: "When [the field commanders] agreed to the creation of a General Reserve they were surrendering, perhaps without realizing it their objections to an Inter-Allied commander-in-chief."[15]

Bliss sensed the political considerations which threatened the future of the General Reserve. He suggested that the subject should not be emphasized in the American press. Opposition, he noted, was strong in Britain, and a similar situation might develop in the United States.[16] Bliss backed the General Reserve not because he thought it an adequate provision against disaster in France but because it seemed to him the best solution to the problem of command that could be achieved, given the delicate political conditions which then existed. Lloyd George had weakened but not eliminated the opposition of his principal military advisors.

The Executive War Board wasted no time making its recommendations to the commanders-in-chief of the various armies. By 6 February the Board approved the text of a letter to be sent to Haig, Pétain, and Diaz (the Italian commander). The letter called for contributions of fourteen French, ten British, and seven Italian divisions. These forces would be concentrated at appropriate locations behind the French and Italian fronts. Haste was necessary due to the imminence of the expected German offensive. Despite yeoman labors, events conspired to frustrate the ambitious plans of the Executive War Board.[17]

FAILURE OF THE GENERAL RESERVE

The surface unity of the Allies was seriously ruffled when the long-concealed disagreements between Lloyd George and General Robertson were aired publicly in February 1918. Robertson attempted to frustrate the Executive War Board by contending that limitations imposed by the British constitution precluded the issuance of orders to the British army by any other person than himself. This specious argument posed the larger issues which divided the Chief of the Imperial General Staff and his Prime Minister. The Parliamentary Opposition precipitated a long cabinet crisis during the period 8-19 February. After a hard struggle, Lloyd George again managed to sustain his authority and Robertson was forced to resign. General Sir Henry Wilson became the new C.I.G.S., but Field Marshal Haig retained command of the British Expeditionary Forces.[18]

These events influenced General Bliss markedly. During his earlier visit to Europe with the House Mission he had been critical of the European statesmen and had absorbed military objections to political meddling with the armies in the field. The behavior of General Robertson convinced him that his original assumptions had been incorrect. He realized that Robertson had raised the constitutional issue only to cover his opposition to a French commander.[19] Bliss believed that political stability in Europe was vital to victory. Writing to Secretary Baker, he said: "Both [Clemenceau] and Lloyd George may be unsafe administrators in time of peace, (I do not know), but for present purposes they are the men for their places." The people trusted them, he concluded, despite the attempts of a "certain clique" to destroy the confidence of the rank and file in Lloyd George.[20] Bliss' awareness that political considerations affected strategic decisions continued to influence his actions, although he assiduously avoided political entanglements in order to accord with the policy of his government.

Ultimately Field Marshal Haig frustrated the success of the General Reserve by refusing to contribute his quota of divisions, although both he and Pétain had agreed to cooperate. Instead, Haig planned to make an agreement with Pétain which would guarantee the protection of the Franco-British front.[21] Haig had discovered that Clemenceau was by no means enthusiastic about the General Reserve. Pétain had impressed the Premier with his arguments against it. Some authorities believe the anticlerical Clemenceau resented the devout Catholicism of General Foch, whose brother was an important churchman. Others think Clemenceau harbored personal military ambitions and sought the command of the Allied armies for himself. In any case Pétain and Haig seized on Clemenceau's recalcitrance to frustrate the General Reserve by the mere expedient of refusing to contribute troops.[22] Lloyd George, still in political difficulties after the resignation of Robertson, did not feel himself strong enough to discharge Haig.

The Executive War Board threatened to resign in an attempt to coerce Haig into cooperation.[23] When Haig stood his ground, the Board passed a resolution on 8 March recommending its own dissolution.[24] The General Reserve was dead.

Unwilling to accept this *fait accompli,* General Bliss labored mightily to resuscitate the General Reserve. He asked the War Department to obtain a statement from President Wilson supporting the continuance of the Executive War Board.[25] The President then sent a message to the American ambassador in London, Walter Hines Page, which asked for the maintenance of the principle of the General Reserve and for contributions of divisions by the armies able to make them.[26] In letters to General Rawlinson (the British military representative) and to the Executive War Board, Bliss pointed out the weaknesses of the Haig-Pétain plans for mutual support: "If all fronts are hard pressed, the Commander-in-Chief who seriously needs assistance will find that he has been relying on a broken reed in placing his trust in this agreement." [27] Bliss believed that in the heat of battle neither Haig nor Pétain would be willing to surrender troops to the other. He strongly resisted the imputation that the commanders-in-chief of the several Entente armies could veto the actions of the Executive War Board. He thought the Board a superior authority because it derived its powers from the Supreme War Council.[28]

Despite Bliss' efforts, the Supreme War Council quietly sidetracked the General Reserve during its fourth session (14-15 March 1918). Lloyd George acknowledged defeat on the issue, realizing he could do nothing further.[29] The strongly expressed message from President Wilson could not be completely ignored, and the Council passed an empty resolution giving lip service to the principle.[30] After Foch became Allied commander-in-chief, the Executive War Board was formally dissolved.[31]

General Bliss' attempt to continue the General Reserve accorded with the American policy of supporting projects intended to improve military coordination on the Western Front which did not require political commitments. Fortunately for the Allies, the failure of the General Reserve did much to prepare the way for the acceptance of a unified command in the wake of the supreme military crisis which soon developed in France.

THE APPOINTMENT OF FOCH AS GENERALISSIMO

On 21 March the long-anticipated German offensive commenced. The initial blow, which struck at the junction of the French and British lines, routed the British Fifth Army. The dimensions of the catastrophe enabled Lloyd George to condone the appointment of a French general to command all the Allied troops in France.[32] Haig experienced a change of heart after Pétain refused to reinforce the beleaguered Fifth Army. As Bliss had predicted, Pétain thought the main effort of the Germans would come in the French sector, and the French commander would not relinquish his reserve.[33] When Haig realized that Pétain had reneged, he summoned Sir Henry Wilson to the front in order to arrange a supreme command.[34]

Haig, Pétain, Foch, and Wilson conferred with Premier Clemenceau and Lord Milner at Doullens on 26 March in order to discuss unity of command. The United States was not represented at this conference. Foch received authority to coordinate the action of the French and British armies by consultation and advice. The Doullens Agreement did not establish unity of command, but it represented a distinct step in that direction.[35] Clemenceau, with considerable lack of grace, finally agreed to support Foch.[36]

Although neither Bliss nor Pershing was present at Doullens, the American government welcomed the prospect of a command arrangement that promised to be far more efficient than the General Reserve. The policy of complete support for unity of command had been vindicated by events.

General Foch was dissatisfied with the Doullens Agreement because it did not confer actual command authority. He could direct the movement of the Allied armies only through consultations with Haig and Pétain. In addition, the Doullens Agreement did not cover the A.E.F., although Pershing theatrically offered his troops for what he termed the "greatest battle in history," and President Wilson cabled congratulations to Foch.[37] Foch began his work energetically, but he pressed strongly for an extension of his authority.[38]

This grant was made at the Beauvais Conference on 3 April. Bliss and Pershing both attended this meeting and supported Foch. They insisted on placing the A.E.F. under the supreme command.[39] The Beauvais Agreement allowed Foch to determine inter-Allied strategy on the Western Front and reserved tactical command to the separate national commanders. The last sentence of the Agreement gave each commander the right to appeal to his government if "the safety of his army is compromised by any order received from General Foch." [40] General Bliss opposed the right of appeal, thus demonstrating his belief that Foch's command if anything should have been stronger.[41] This action was consistent with the previous attitude of the American government.

The final step in the evolution of Foch's command was taken at Abbeville during the fifth session of the Supreme War Council on 1-2 May. Premier Orlando of Italy agreed to allow Foch to "coordinate" the movements of the Italian army but refused to grant full authority until Allied forces fought in Italy under the same conditions as in France.[42]

Although General Foch received his powers from special conferences rather than from the Supreme War Council, the previous activities of the latter organ had helped greatly to prepare the way for the supreme command. The Council provided a forum for those who believed that unity of command was a prerequisite to victory. Clemenceau's inconstancy had frustrated the General Reserve, but the German offensive was sufficiently disturbing to convince hesitant leaders that unity of command could be postponed no longer. Events forced the very arrangement for which the American government had contended. American pressure played an important role in the events which culminated in the elevation of Foch. The unified command seemed to improve inter-Allied military potential without requiring any apparent political involvements.

THE EFFECT OF FOCH'S COMMAND ON THE SUPREME WAR COUNCIL

The Supreme War Council had been established to concert inter-Allied military operations by methods short of a unified command. Once Foch assumed command of the Allied armies, the Council seemed to lose much of its *raison d'être.* The military representatives no longer prepared strategic recommendations pertaining to the Western Front. They became increasingly concerned with logistical problems. The political functions of the Council remained unimpaired, but this fact was somewhat obscured at the time because all attention had been drawn to the great battles in France. Foch's authority was confined to the Western Front. The Supreme War Council concerned itself in the later phases of the war with political-military questions pertaining to other theaters. The military representatives busied themselves with strategy in the secondary theaters and continued to study supply problems.

Colonel House began to receive information relating to the adverse effect of Foch's command on the Council. His informant in Paris, Arthur Frazier, told him that observers in Europe thought the Council had "suffered eclipse." [43] Sir William Wiseman, then visiting in Europe, also commented on the changed status of the Council, particularly as it affected the military representatives:

> Position of the Supreme War Council at Versailles is unsatisfactory. I feel that this body properly constituted and used might be the solution of many difficulties. In the meantime they are doing very useful work, but no one pays any attention to their recommendations. [Bliss] feels this situation keenly. He has achieved a considerable success and represented America with distinction and dignity. Unfortunately he and [Pershing] do not get on well together.[44]

Despite the promotion of Foch, the Allies continued to suffer serious defeats in France. Colonel House began to consider changes in the functions of the military representatives in order to enhance the effectiveness of the unified command. He thought the recent defeats of the Allies should not have occurred and concluded that the fault lay with the higher command of the national armies. He wanted to clip the wings of Haig, Pétain, and Pershing. Writing to the President early in June, he maintained that "Foch should build up the military end of the Supreme War Council and use it as an important part of the General Staff. It amounts to next to nothing now." After further thought, he wrote to Bliss in the same vein.[45]

General Bliss did not agree with the Colonel. Waiting over a month to reply, he said that his views concerning the Supreme War Council had altered since his return to Europe: "I am now convinced that the true function of the Supreme War Council is the determination of questions of policy upon which all of the Allies can agree." The proper duty of the military representatives was to propose methods of coordinating military operations on all fronts rather than to develop detailed strategic, logistical, and tactical plans for specific theaters. He believed the meetings of the Supreme War Council created inter-Allied harmony that otherwise would have been difficult to achieve. He rejected House's suggestion that the military representatives serve as an inter-Allied general staff for Foch. In such conditions:

> The Supreme War Council would make itself, literally, the Commander-in-Chief of the Armies in the field and responsible for all of the details of the execution of the campaign. I feel sure that our Allies would not consent to such an arrangement.[46]

Colonel House's suggestions demonstrated once again that American political leaders conceived of the Supreme War Council narrowly, assuming that its principal function was to produce detailed military plans. House ignored its diplomatic capabilities, but Bliss came to entertain much broader views. Whereas House wanted the military representatives to plan detailed campaigns and issue orders to commanders in the field, Bliss wanted the Council to draw up broad directives in accord with the political situation, taking into account the advice of the military counsellors.

Tension between the British and the French further complicated the affairs of the Council after the appointment of Foch. Lloyd George and General Wilson feared French domination of inter-Allied planning. The British leaders wanted to insure the continuation of the Supreme War Council through which Britain could maintain its proper influence over decisions. A report by Lieutenant Colonel L. S. Amery, head of the Political Branch of the British Section, reflected British anxieties. Amery defined Foch's powers narrowly, arguing that he merely replaced the Executive War Board and that he controlled only the Western Front. He believed the need for a supranational group to study the military situation "from the point of view of the Allies as a whole . . . is just as great as ever." He recommended the creation of a board of political representatives, similar to the board of military representatives, which could draw up a "common general policy" for diplomatic as well as military action. If the Allies failed to coordinate their policy, he believed they would be "at as great a disadvantage in negotiation as they have lately been in strategy." [47]

General Bliss soon noted that the British feared French domination. Reporting to Secretary Baker late in June, he placed his finger directly on the sore point:

> The British lay more stress than anyone else on the functions of the Supreme War Council. . . . The British are very anxious to retain it, among other reasons, doubtless, because of the bad moral effect of its being broken up. Of course there is only one power that would think it could gain any advantage by the dissolution of the Supreme War Council. M. Clemenceau wants to put the whole direction of the war in all theatres in the hands of General Foch. I do not think the British will stand for this for a moment. If they will not, that of itself, makes the retention of the War Council a necessity.[48]

A British attempt to curtail supposed French ambitions took place during the seventh session of the Supreme War Council in July. This episode is discussed in Chapter 7.

Foch's assumption of supreme command had resulted in differing responses from the principal members of the Western coalition. Italy refused to expand Foch's authority to the Italian front, permitting him only the power to "coordinate" Italian movements with operations in France. Britain sought to sustain the authority of the Council in order to protect against French dominance of inter-Allied strategy. France hoped to expand Foch's authority, thus minimizing the importance of the Council. The United States continued to advocate improvements in unity of plan, control, and command, wishing to facilitate inter-Allied cooperation.

The Supreme War Council concerted an important measure of unity prior to the establishment of the unified command, a fact which smoothed the way for the appointment of Foch after the German offensive of March 1918. The negotiations concerning the General Reserve brought the issue of command to the fore and tended to discredit nationalistic rivalries and jealousies. The role of the Supreme War Council in preparing for the establishment of the unified command was one of its most significant contributions to victory.

The functions of General Foch lessened the prestige of the Supreme War Council and the influence of the military representatives, a development which met with opposition in Britain and America. After Foch assumed his command, the Council and its military representatives concentrated on affairs in secondary theaters and massive logistical problems. As the war moved toward its climax, political matters claimed increasing attention.

The continual diversion of inter-Allied effort resulting from divided authority convinced American leaders that unity of command was necessary to victory, and General Bliss never swerved in his advocacy of improved coordination. As time passed, Bliss came to believe that the Council should coordinate broad political-military strategy rather than plan and direct specific campaigns, but the United States government continued to oppose political activity by the Council.

CHAPTER 5

Utilization of American Manpower

THE need for American manpower to bolster the Entente armies became manifest as the Allied military position deteriorated during the latter months of 1917. When the Allied missions had visited Washington, their members had urged amalgamation of American troops into the Entente armies, but the United States government had decided to equip, train, and employ an independent force. The Entente Powers had advocated amalgamation because they feared the United States could not field an independent army quickly enough to influence the outcome of the war. During the period of urgency which followed upon the Allied disasters of 1917, the practice of amalgamation seemed peculiarly logical to harassed statesmen and soldiers in France and Britain.

Paradoxically, the decline in the military fortunes of the Western coalition strengthened not only the Allied demand for amalgamation but also the American determination to field an independent army. The United States was just as aware as the Allies that many American soldiers would have to be sent to Europe. The bone of contention was the manner in which reinforcements would be utilized in France. Fearful of a great German effort against their depleted formations during 1918, the Allies believed American troops could make a significant contribution only if placed under the command of European officers and in the company of battle-hardened French and British troops. The American leaders, fearful of dividing their forces, believed their soldiers might fight in vain unless American power were brought to bear on the Western Front in the form of a national army.

The Allies sought to gain American acceptance of amalgamation by means of negotiations at the Supreme War Council. These exchanges cast further light on the nature of political-military relationships within the Western coalition.

BACKGROUND OF THE DISPUTE OVER AMALGAMATION

Long before the Paris Conference late in 1917, the Allies became alarmed by the seeming slowness of the American mobilization.[1] Its deliberate pace, imposed by the desire to build a self-sufficient organization, began to frighten the Allies, who were then becoming aware of the German build-up for a great offensive in 1918. During the stay of the House Mission in Europe the British renewed their pressure for some form of amalgamation. They asked for temporary amalgamation during the crisis which impended, realizing that permanent absorption of American fighting men would bruise American sensitivities unduly. Pershing and House resisted this revival of earlier proposals and decided that the preparation of an independent army should continue.[2]

This decision was not born of ignorance; everyone knew that a great German attack would take place in France and that a massive American effort would be needed to stem the tide.[3] Colonel House recognized the desperate need for a prompt and powerful reinforcement, but he suspected that amalgamation would create undue friction between Allied and American troops and that American soldiers so employed might never be returned to General Pershing's command. In addition, a policy of amalgamation might obscure the military contributions of the United States to victory.[4] Pershing sustained his pressure for expanded troop shipments to France but strongly opposed amalgamation. To strengthen his case, he pointed out that troops from the nations of the British Commonwealth had never been integrated into the British army but had fought with distinction as separate units.[5] Despite continuing pressure, the United States avoided binding commitments.[6]

On 18 December 1917 Secretary Baker sent instructions to Pershing which governed the American attitude towards amalgamation throughout the long controversy to come:

> Both English and French are pressing upon the President their desire to have your forces amalgamated with theirs by regiments and companies and both express belief in impending heavy drive by Germans somewhere along the line of the Western Front. We do not desire loss of identity of our forces but regard that as secondary to the meeting of any critical situation by the most helpful use possible of the troops at your command. . . . The President . . . wishes you to have full authority to use the troops at your command as you deem wise in consultation with the French and British commanders in chief. . . . The President's whole purpose [is] to acquaint you with the representations made here and to authorize you to act with entire freedom in making the best disposition and use of your forces possible to accomplish the main purposes in view.[7]

The moderate tone of this cable reflected the desire of the

government to cooperate with the Allies but also the wish to avoid meddling with the commander in the field. The government did not favor amalgamation but had not taken a definitive stand against it, should conditions require its adoption.

Both President Wilson and Secretary Baker wished to avoid interference with Pershing's rightful prerogatives. They habitually deferred to professional military counsel in situations which did not seem to require political participation. They hoped to avoid repeating what they believed to have been unfortunate political interference with commanders in the field during previous American wars. The views of General Pershing and his staff consequently had great weight in determining the future course of the controversy over amalgamation.

For reasons of its own, the French government assumed that Pershing had orders to proceed with amalgamation. Pétain urged immediate amalgamation, but Pershing refused to cooperate.[8] Highly irritated, President Raymond Poincaré in late December 1917 wrote a personal letter to President Wilson calling forcefully for amalgamation. "The turning into practice of your decision," he said, "has unluckily met, up to now, with some difficulty, and an agreement has not proved possible between [Pétain] and Pershing."[9] Thus began the sustained Allied criticism of General Pershing which endured throughout the war. Pershing's reaction was to express the attitude he clung to relentlessly during 1918:

> I [have] expressed a willingness to aid in any way in an emergency but do not think good reason yet exists for us to break up our own divisions and scatter regiments for service among the French and British, especially under the guise of instruction. As we are now at war ourselves the integrity of our own forces should be preserved as far as

> possible. . . . The President and the Secretary of War may depend on it that every endeavor will be made to arrive at satisfactory agreements consistent with maintenance of our own national military identity.[10]

Pershing and his staff firmly believed the United States could make its best contribution to the war by building an independent army. They thought American power would be dispersed and wasted if amalgamation took place.[11] Undoubtedly personal ambitions and national pride subtly moved them, but Pershing also attached great importance to a political consideration which also must have influenced his government:

> We must look forward to bearing a very heavy part in this conflict before it ends, and our forces should not be dissipated for a temporary emergency. Moreover, it is unnecessary to say, when the war ends, our position will be stronger if our army acting as such shall have played a distinct and definite part.[12]

This point of view does not appear to have been the most important element in fixing American attitudes, but it was certainly a significant aspect of the controversy. Pershing's staff officers were especially attracted by it. General Fox Conner, the Operations Officer (G-3), included it among other arguments in staff papers concerning the subject.[13]

The greatest obstacle to the creation of an independent American army in France was the shortage of shipping. The United States had launched a huge program of maritime construction, but this effort could not be expected to provide adequate tonnage for some time to come. Only the British possessed enough ships to meet minimal needs.[14] As the controversy over amalgamation developed, it became clear that the British hoped to barter tonnage in return for American acceptance of amalgamation. Pershing was forced to strike periodic bargains with the British in order to obtain ships for the transportation of American soldiers to Europe. His bargaining power was strong because the need for American troops was so great, but he found he could not resist amalgamation without encountering a British tendency to withhold shipping.

Early in January the Supreme War Council began to consider amalgamation. On 8 January the President replied to Poincaré's letter, assuring him that the United States was seriously concerned with the problem of utilizing American manpower properly. He told his French counterpart that General Bliss, then on his way to Versailles, would place the issue before the Supreme War Council for full and frank discussion. "The judgment of the Council with regard to it will, I need hardly assure you, be conclusively influential with the Government of the United States."[15] The President's willingness to accept the decision of the Supreme War Council was not shared by General Pershing. Many acrimonious disputes transpired before the subject ceased to disturb inter-Allied relations.

THE ADOPTION OF THE SIX-DIVISION PROGRAM

Before General Bliss arrived in Europe, General Pershing had tentatively agreed to allow 150 battalions of American infantry to serve temporarily with the British army in order to receive training. After their training ended, they would be regrouped into regiments and returned to American command. Presumably the British would not use them in combat. The reinforcement of 150 battalions would be an addition to the number of American troops originally scheduled for shipment to Europe during the early months of 1918. Consequently the training program would eventually augment General Pershing's build-up. After the British War Cabinet approved the plan, General Robertson asked Haig to support it.[16] The "150-battalion plan" drew support because it promised to reinforce British formations at least temporarily during a critical period without materially disturbing the American build-up. It required the British to enlarge the amount of shipping they planned to allocate to the United States.

Pershing asked the War Department to send relatively untrained units to the British, reserving more advanced troops for his own purposes. He could then receive and train artillery, signal, ordnance, and other supporting components which he could unite with the 150 battalions of infantry on their return from the British in order to form complete divisions.[17] Pershing consistently struggled to develop a "balanced force" by fitting his shipping schedule to his personnel requirements.

Although President Wilson approved the 150-battalion plan, he was disposed to distrust British promises to provide additional shipping. Baker emphasized that Pershing had accepted the plan contingent on the contribution of increased tonnage.[18] The President grasped the connection between British shipping and American manpower and cautioned the Secretary of War to watch the British carefully:

> I have one fear about this [the 150-battalion plan]. It is that, whatever they may promise now, the British will, when it comes to the pinch, in fact cut us out from some of the tonnage they will promise us for our general program in order themselves to make sure of these battalions; or will promise us less for the general program than they would otherwise have given.[19]

This frank manifestation of distrust reflected an important tendency in American thinking which naturally strengthened General Pershing's hand. Bliss was enjoined to prevent reductions in the shipping originally contemplated for the United States and was cautioned to rebuff restrictions on Pershing's right to recall his troops from the British at pleasure.[20] American policy was now fixed. The United States government opposed amalgamation and would not consider such proposals unless the British provided additional transport for the shipment of American troops to Europe. The American commander was to retain authority to recall troops loaned temporarily to the Allies whenever he wished to do so.

General Pershing had seemed to accept the 150-battalion plan provided it did not interfere with the development of an independent American army, and General Bliss arrived in Europe under the impression that the proposal had been approved in principle.[21] Soon after his appearance in Paris, he conferred with Pershing, Haig and Pétain and supported the 150-battalion plan, only to discover later from the irate Pershing that the American commander still objected to it. Pershing stressed to Bliss the necessity of presenting a united front when dealing with the Entente soldiers.[22] Thenceforth Bliss carefully ascertained the exact state of Pershing's opinions before venturing to express his views on matters concerning the A.E.F.[23] The American military representative's willingness generally to defer to Pershing's judgment, even when his personal views differed widely, eliminated a source of potential strife.

Pershing's renewed opposition to the 150-battalion plan and Britain's hesitation to provide additional shipping brought about further inter-Allied negotiations which culminated in the adoption of the "six-division plan." Britain promised to transport six complete infantry divisions to Europe, to be temporarily integrated into the British army for training. This arrangement did not disturb Pershing's plans for developing a balanced force.

Lloyd George reluctantly agreed to the new proposal after a vain effort to break down the concerted resistance of Pershing and Bliss.[24]

The six-division program came before the second session of the Supreme War Council on 30 January. During formal debate Haig and Pétain pleaded for immediate incorporation of American troops into their commands, the latter emphasizing his belief that otherwise American troops would make no contribution of significance to the 1918 campaign.[25] Pershing then countered with a forceful argument against the Anglo-French position. National sentiment in the United States strongly opposed amalgamation, he said, and its adoption might cause unfortunate political repercussions. Differences in national character would create friction among the troops. The effort and direction of the American drive would be dissipated. Additional manpower could be found without resorting to amalgamation. Pershing thus directly contradicted Pétain and Haig, but he offered to permit temporary amalgamation for training purposes only.[26] This concession was an empty gesture because he intended to withdraw the troops as soon as they were trained, in order to form them into complete divisions under American commanders. Pershing hoped to destroy European illusions that he would consent to permanent amalgamation.

General Bliss reiterated the American attitude in accents quite as sweeping as those of Pershing. Citing the Anglo-American negotiations which had produced the six-division program, he defended the previous arrangements and minimized the need for permanent amalgamation. He wanted it clearly understood that the training of American troops by the Allied armies would be regarded merely as a stepping stone to the formation of an American army. "Such a thing as permanent amalgamation of our units with the French and British units," he concluded, "would be intolerable to American sentiment."[27] The Allies finally conceded the point and settled on the six-division program.[28]

President Wilson provided constant political support for Pershing, holding to his policy of noninterference with military decisions. Nothing, he believed, should be allowed to interfere with the creation of a huge and independent American army. The Congress had been conducting an investigation of the War Department based on the seeming slowness of the American build-up. The President feared that amalgamation might lend substance to the criticism of his political opponents.[29] Secretary Baker, under severe attack in the Congress, also hardened his opposition to amalgamation.[30]

The Entente could not afford to antagonize the President because everything seemed to turn on the American reinforcement. General Bliss cogently described the prevailing mood in Europe:

> I doubt if I could make anyone not present at the recent meetings of the Supreme War Council realize the anxiety and fear that pervades the minds of political and military men here. . . . They openly state that their hope is in the man-power of the United States.[31]

Bliss was by no means as opposed to amalgamation as was Pershing, although he loyally supported his colleague. He believed that the military situation could be retrieved if American troops arrived on time in France. He conceded privately that amalgamation might become necessary. He thought the British would supply urgently needed shipping if they received troops in return. The possibility of future disagreements between the American military representative and the commander of the A.E.F. thus developed as the Allies braced for the German assault.

THE IMPACT OF THE GERMAN OFFENSIVE

After the third session of the Supreme War Council, Pershing not only sustained his opposition to amalgamation but also began to press for the delineation of an American sector on the French front.[32] His extensive preparations naturally stiffened the American determination to establish an independent army. It tended to foreclose Allied objections. For the moment, the controversy over amalgamation ceased to ruffle inter-Allied relations.

This interlude did not endure for long. The great German attack of 21 March 1918 immediately revived proposals to institute amalgamation for combat as well as for training. Lloyd George seized the opportunity to make a strong plea for amalgamation through his ambassador in Washington, the capable Lord Reading. Secretary Baker was then in London, making his first tour of inspection to the combat zone, and Lloyd George made personal representations to him.[33] At the same time Lord Reading sought to impress Colonel House with the dangers of the situation in France. He estimated that Britain could provide enough tonnage to transport 120,000 American troops per month to France during the period April-July, a total of half a million, if the United States would allow their amalgamation into the Entente armies.[34] Under the impact of the German attack, Pershing altered his policy to the extent of using some of his units to relieve French divisions guarding quiet sectors of the front. The veteran French divisions then reinforced the threatened sectors under attack.[35] This movement delayed the concentration of American divisions in a sector near the Saint-Mihiel salient, where Pershing intended to launch the first American offensive.

The permanent military representatives had not been idle during the crisis. General Rawlinson, the British representative at this time, drafted a joint note urging the United States to accept temporary amalgamation until the German attack had been contained. The note proposed to transport infantry and machine-gun units only during the emergency. This procedure would certainly frustrate Pershing's efforts to build a balanced force capable of independent action. The American general forcefully refused to accept the plan. Discussing the subject on 27 March with the military representatives, Pershing began by noting that his previous arrangements with the French and the British were progressing satisfactorily. He would permit the infantry and machine-gun units of the six divisions then being shipped to Europe under the six-division program to precede their supporting elements, but he would agree to nothing else. After Pershing left the meeting, General Bliss gave vent to a rare display of anger. He stressed that "General Pershing expressed only his personal opinion and . . . it is the Military Representatives who must make a decision." [36] The group approved Joint Note No. 18, which included the substance of Rawlinson's plan.[37] Pershing then inaugurated a studied effort to undermine the implementation of Joint Note No. 18.[38]

General Bliss had been deeply impressed by the strength of the German attacks and the weakness of the Allies. The failure of the General Reserve seemed to call for important changes in policy. He and Pershing had concurred in supporting unity of command, but they differed widely on the issue of amalgamation. Bliss was now willing to acquiesce in a temporary scheme of amalgamation which far exceeded the wishes of Pershing. He supported Joint Note No. 18 not only because of his personal opinion but because to do otherwise would have undermined the prestige of the Supreme War Council and its military representatives.

Secretary Baker hastened to Paris, and after consultations with Pershing and Bliss he drew up an important message to President Wilson on the subject of amalgamation. Baker called for acceptance of Joint Note No. 18, but he recommended certain crippling reservations which lessened the force of the military representatives' proposals. Baker did not want to oppose General Pershing, but he recognized the force of Bliss' contentions. Consequently he attempted to straddle. "We must keep in mind the formation of an American army, while, at the same time, we must not seem to sacrifice joint efficiency at a critical moment." He proposed the following language for the President's use in his reply to the Supreme War Council:

> The purpose of the American Government is to render the fullest cooperation and aid and therefore . . . the preferential transportation of American infantry and machine-gun units in the present emergency is approved. Such units when transported will be under the direction of the Commander-in-Chief of the American Expeditionary Forces and will be assigned for training and use by him in his discretion. He will use these and all other troops under his command in such manner as to render the greatest military assistance, keeping in mind always the determination of his Government to have its various military forces collected, as speedily as their training and military situation permit, into an independent American army. . . . All arrangements made by him for their temporary training and service will be made with that end in view.[39]

Despite the protestation of willingness to cooperate, the Baker message did not envision a real change in American plans. It revised the schedule of troop shipments, but it did not preclude the eventual formation of an independent army. Pershing retained full authority to recall American troops attached to other armies at his pleasure.

The President immediately accepted Baker's recommendation and gave the Secretary full power to make all necessary decisions during the crisis in France.[40] Pershing, Bliss, and Baker now assumed that the United States was bound merely to transport immediately the combat elements of the six divisions previously allocated for training with the British army.[41] The British wanted American troops to fight as well as to train with their units. Dissatisfied with the Baker plan, the Allies turned their attention to Washington.[42]

Under instructions from Lloyd George, Lord Reading obtained an audience with President Wilson in order to urge a broad project of amalgamation. Emerging from this conference, the British Ambassador interpreted the President's rather general remarks to mean that the United States had altered its policy. He thought the President had agreed to permit the shipment of 120,000 combat troops a month for the period April-July to be incorporated into the French and British armies.[43] Baker first heard of the Wilson-Reading conversation from Lloyd George on 3 April. The War Department sent a cable which seemed to confirm a change in policy. Baker, alarmed, requested clarification.[44] A quick reply from the President said that he had merely accepted the formula suggested by Baker, leaving the details to future negotiation.[45]

Reading was immediately informed that he had misinterpreted the President's remarks. When the British Ambassador again approached the President, he found him unwilling to take further action until he had conferred with Baker. The latter was making his return voyage from Europe.[46] Hoping to regain the initiative, the British attempted to achieve their purposes by emphasizing the assumed difference of opinion between the President and his military advisors, but this tactic did not succeed.[47]

Pershing then developed a rather heavy-handed

stratagem by which he appeared to concede something to the Allies without materially affecting his build-up. Revising his shipping schedules, he arranged to transport combat units and supporting echelons to Europe in alternating waves. The combat troops would serve temporarily for training purposes with the British or the French but would soon be withdrawn and re-formed into complete divisions with their support when another wave of combat troops arrived. The second wave of front-line troops would then be sent to the Allies for training. In short, the General wanted to utilize the British and French armies as training cadres for his troops, but he had no intention of permitting his men to fight under a foreign flag except in dire emergency.[48]

Although Pershing remained intractable, the constant British importunities evoked some sympathy among American leaders. Colonel House, always sensitive to European opinion, sympathized with Pershing's desire to build up the American army, but he recommended a change in policy to meet the wishes of the Allies. "The thing to be done now," he told the President, "is to stop the Germans and to stop them it is evident that we must put in every man that is available." [49] General Bliss continued to reflect his predilection for some form of temporary amalgamation. Writing to Baker, he propounded his view forcefully:

> I do not propose to make the United States a recruiting ground to fill up the ranks of the British and French armies. I only propose to put our troops into their large organizations . . . and then form our Divisions into American Corps and American Armies serving with the British or French as the case may be, but without an independent system of supply and without an independent service-of-the-rear. We will then get into the war far more quickly, far more efficiently, and with far less cost.[50]

Bliss did not criticize Pershing publicly, but privately he advocated a policy distinctly opposed to that of the Commander of the A.E.F. Bliss spoke from an inter-Allied perspective, Pershing from a somewhat restricted national point of view. The latter's stubborn attitude engendered increasing irritation among Allied leaders.[51]

The persistent negotiations of Lord Reading finally resulted in a limited agreement to permit the transport of 120,000 American troops per month to Europe for an indefinite period. Under the terms of the "Baker Memorandum" of 21 April, Pershing retained the right to withdraw American troops from the Allied armies as he desired. Lloyd George accepted the Baker Memorandum with alacrity.[52]

Unaware of the activity in Washington, Pershing had proceeded to London in order to make his own arrangement with the British. He was immediately confronted with the Baker Memorandum and had to make limited concessions. The result was the "Pershing-Milner Agreement." He decided to allow the temporary amalgamation of the combat elements of six American divisions during May for training purposes only. Extra British shipping which might become available was to be utilized for the transport of troops specified by the United States. Both countries understood that complete American divisions would be formed at an early date.[53]

After returning to France, Pershing conferred with General Foch, who pressed him to extend the Pershing-Milner Agreement to June and July. Foch paid lip service to the creation of an independent American army but frankly admitted his belief that during the emergency only combat troops should be shipped to France.[54] Pershing remained unconvinced, but he was sufficiently impressed by the German threat to recommend to the War Department an immediate draft of 1,500,000 men for shipment to France as soon as possible. The War Department rejected this proposal, primarily because their training cantonments could not accommodate so many men. The Department continued to maintain the draft at its maximum and to train all types of troops in the United States.[55]

When the terms of the Pershing-Milner Agreement reached Washington, Lord Reading realized that Pershing had outmaneuvered him. When the British Ambassador complained to Baker, the Secretary of War put him off and reported the confused situation to the President.[56] Baker sacrificed his arrangement with Reading and accepted the Pershing-Milner Agreement, thus reverting to his customary practice of supporting General Pershing's desires. Wishing to minimize Allied influence over the American reinforcement, he told Bliss: "I prefer to follow the recommendations of the Versailles conference [Joint Note No. 18] as a matter of choice, rather than [as] a matter of promise to Great Britain." [57]

The French government further confused the complicated situation by objecting strongly to the Pershing-Milner Agreement. During a special meeting at Abbeville on 27 April, Clemenceau complained bitterly because the arrangement did not allocate any Americans to the French army for training. His protest forced the conference to recommend reconsideration of the Pershing-Milner Agreement at the imminent meeting of the Supreme War Council. As a parting shot, Clemenceau urged the dispatch of a joint Anglo-French commission to Washington in order to force a clear-cut American commitment.[58] The failure of France and Britain to present a united front to the United States appreciably strengthened Pershing's hand.

Up to this point the Supreme War Council had performed important but limited services in connection with the controversy over amalgamation. It had participated in the negotiations which produced the six-division program. The military representatives had precipitated the controversies of April by approving Joint Note No. 18. The United States had weakened the potential influence of the Supreme War Council by giving General Pershing the power to control the training and employment of the American army. Pershing bypassed the Council by negotiating with individual representatives of the Allied governments. The General's intransigence forced Britain and France to initiate direct negotiations in Washington, a circumstance which added to the confusion. Although General Bliss favored limited concessions in order to meet the emergency in France, he had to support Pershing at Versailles.

Clemenceau's angry protest placed the problems of amalgamation directly in the hands of the Supreme War Council. This change of practice led to firm agreements, well known and generally accepted, despite the differences in outlook which so complicated discussions. Had this step been taken earlier, it is likely that the controversy would not have become so acrimonious and that faster and more effective action might have resulted without stirring up so much rancor. When the Supreme War Council convened at Abbeville for its fifth session on 1 May, the group achieved an important clarification of the policy for training and employing the American army.

THE SUPREME WAR COUNCIL AND AMALGAMATION, MAY-JULY 1918

Clemenceau began the fifth session of the Council with a bitter attack on the Pershing-Milner Agreement. Both Pershing and Milner rejected the Tiger's criticisms. Seeking a compromise, Lloyd George maintained that the

American army could begin to operate as an independent element by September or October even if, for the moment, the United States agreed to transport only combat troops to France. This phase could be followed by another which concentrated on the shipment of services-of-the-rear and headquarters troops. Foch then revived the controversy by maintaining that the Pershing-Milner Agreement impinged upon his command prerogatives. Clemenceau closed the day's discussion by insisting on the suspension of the Pershing-Milner Agreement and the negotiation of an entirely new arrangement.[59]

The next day Lloyd George again assumed the mantle of compromise, expressing his belief that both creation of the American army and reinforcement of the Allied armies could be accomplished without undue delay. Foch reiterated his arguments for the transport of at least 120,000 combat troops per month for the period May-July. Under great pressure, Pershing finally accepted an arrangement which placated the Allies. It ratified the policy of building an independent American army, accepted the Pershing-Milner Agreement for May, included a similar provision for June, and postponed the July settlement until the June session of the Supreme War Council.[60] This resolution superseded all previous agreements. No one was completely satisfied, but it represented a distinct success for the Council. The conferees had managed to reach an agreed solution despite the widely divergent views of the participants.

For the moment General Pershing felt secure, especially since his actions at Abbeville were well received in Washington.[61] Baker informed the President that he was "very favorably impressed" by Pershing's attitude and received a reply which concurred in this sentiment.[62] Baker also notified Bliss of his satisfaction, seeking gracefully to inform the military representative that Pershing's views had found favor in Washington:

> We must continue to be guided by [Pershing's] judgment of the military exigencies in France. . . . This, of course, is only just to General Pershing, upon whom the responsibility for our military operations rests, and it obviates the possibility of trying to settle the same questions in two places at the same time, with discordant settlements as a result.[63]

Bliss replied that he always supported Pershing publicly, but in the same letter he did not hesitate to condemn the Commander-in-Chief's attitude. Foch, he said, was the supreme commander and deserved unswerving support, but Pershing, a subordinate officer, had imposed his will upon the Generalissimo.[64]

Secretary Baker shared President Wilson's irritation with the continual controversies over amalgamation, which stemmed from the failure to direct negotiations into one channel. He first attempted to simplify procedure by concentrating authority in the hands of Pershing, but that officer's attitude was so forbidding that this step foreclosed discussion regardless of merit. The Secretary still hoped to avoid civilian interference with such decisions, even though the Supreme War Council, a civilian agency, sought to assume responsibility for the training and employment of American troops. When Foch inspired attempts to go over Pershing's head directly to Washington, Baker assured the French and British ambassadors that the American government would not contradict the professional judgment of General Pershing.[65]

Despite his continuing support for the American commander, President Wilson's patience was growing thin. He finally directed Baker to suggest a more "sympathetic" attitude to Pershing. Baker's tactful instructions clearly constituted a gentle rebuke.[66] The General was not fooled by Baker's subtlety, and he sent a strong message defending his approach to the hilt. Opposing alteration of the Abbeville Agreement, he said the Allies would continue to clamor for replacements as long as they entertained any hopes of receiving them.[67]

Abandoning their previous restraint, the Allied leaders began to criticize Pershing overtly, and Colonel House received intimations of this development. Sir William Wiseman told him of Pershing's obsession with an autonomous army in terms that implied distinct criticism.[68] House kept the President informed. The Colonel was beginning to suspect that Pershing was incapable of inter-Allied negotiations.[69] When Lloyd George urged the dispatch of House to Europe in order to represent the United States on the Supreme War Council, his move was interpreted as an attempt to curb the power of Pershing. Lord Reading duly mentioned the matter to House, but the Colonel refused to rise to the bait. Notifying the President of the Prime Minister's overture, he said: "Lord Reading confessed to me that he thought it would be a mistake for me to go or for you to send anyone because it is so evident that what Lloyd George wants is someone to overrule Pershing."[70] This episode stemmed an incipient reaction against the General's intransigence, but House still entertained doubts about Pershing.[71]

The latter continued to hasten the creation of an independent army. The American desire to launch their first offensive against the Saint-Mihiel salient required the permission of General Foch. Pershing gained this concession by promising to locate American divisions in quiet sectors of the French front, thus releasing French divisions for service in more troubled areas. In order to gather American troops for this purpose, Pershing planned to recall units then training with the British. The General contemplated a cycle for his units which included basic training in the United States, further instruction with the British, front-line experience in quiet sectors of the French front, and finally offensive combat under American command. This plan served his purposes well, since it granted the shadow of amalgamation but not the substance. The Allies wanted fighting men, not trainees who had to be withheld from combat.[72]

The sixth session of the Supreme War Council, beginning on 1 June, took up the question of shipments of American troops for the month of July. On 2 June the French, British, and American leaders met privately and produced a new agreement providing for greatly augmented shipments of American troops during both June and July. The Allies urged immediate transport of combat troops only, but they weakened their bargaining power by failing to agree among themselves on the disposition of the men. Pershing managed thereby to obtain enough shipping to transport the personnel of complete divisions. The final settlement provided for the transport of 500,000 American soldiers during the period June-July, 310,000 of whom would be infantrymen or machine-gunners. The remainder would be designated by Pershing. Lloyd George sought to gain for Haig the right to determine when Americans training with the British would be returned to Pershing, but the American commander absolutely refused to consider this suggestion. It certainly would have resulted in the loss of much of his command for an extended period.[73]

The concluding sentence of this arrangement, thereafter called the Pershing-Milner-Foch Agreement, summed up the reasons for adopting the policy of shipping relatively untrained troops to Europe during the emergency:

> We recognize that the combatant troops to be despatched in July may have to include troops which have had insufficient training but we consider the present emergency is such as to justify a temporary departure by the United States from sound principles of training especially as a similar course is being followed by France and Great Britain.[74]

The sense of urgency in the text of the Pershing-Milner-Foch Agreement reflected the serious situation which prevailed on the Western Front. The irritation with the United States which prevailed among Allied leaders at this time stemmed to some extent from their feeling that General Pershing had underestimated the seriousness of the crisis.

Lloyd George, Clemenceau, and Orlando chose to emphasize their opinions on the question of amalgamation by sending a letter to President Wilson, noting the difficult situation in France, urging the continued shipment of combat troops only, and indicating that an American army of at least one hundred divisions would be required to establish sufficient numerical superiority over the German army. The tone and phraseology of this communication, although cordial, implied severe criticism of General Pershing.[75] Its ostensible purpose was to bolster the case for the Pershing-Milner-Foch Agreement, but its principal effect was to suggest the curbing of the American commander.[76]

Colonel House, who of all the American leaders was most critical of Pershing, responded to this prod by recommending a sweeping change in Pershing's authority. He sought to transfer Pershing's political powers to others and to limit the General strictly to military matters. Writing to President Wilson immediately after learning of the prime ministers' letter, House stressed the injurious effect of Pershing's attitude on the unified command:

> It is clear that Pershing should confine his activities to the molding [of] our army into an efficient fighting machine and directing it against the enemy. . . .
>
> If Pershing had nothing else to think about I doubt whether he has the capacity to build up a staff adequate to the needs of the occasion. Certainly he can never do it under present conditions. . . .
>
> What I have in mind to suggest to you is that Pershing be relieved from all responsibility except the training and fighting of our troops. All his requirements for equipping and maintaining these troops should be on other shoulders. He should be relieved of all questions of policy except where his opinion is asked. There should be no need for him to be in consultation with the Prime Ministers and Foreign Secretaries. . . . He should be in touch with Foch and Foch should be in touch with these [officials]. Foch should build up the military end of the Supreme War Council and use it as an important part of the General Staff. It amounts to next to nothing now.[77]

House suggested that E. R. Stettinius, one of Baker's most trusted assistants in the War Department, be sent to France to deal with matters of political significance. His earlier opposition to political representation in Europe declined when he became aware that Pershing was thoroughly disliked. House continued to think of inter-Allied cooperation primarily in terms of joint military effort in order to defeat Germany as quickly as possible. His attitudes undoubtedly reflected the opinions filtered to him by Sir William Wiseman.

Secretary Baker at first seemed to oppose the ideas of Colonel House but soon began to express qualified approval.[78] Responding to the President's request for an opinion on House's suggestions, Baker proposed that General George Goethals of Panama Canal fame be sent to assume command of Pershing's services-of-the-rear and that Vance McCormick be dispatched to handle political matters. McCormick had served as national chairman of the Democratic Party and was generally popular in Wilsonian circles. Baker agreed that the unified command needed a boost and that the United States needed a political representative in Europe specifically authorized to deal with inter-Allied questions of a military character.[79]

A month later Baker wrote tactfully to General Pershing, suggesting the appointment of Goethals to command the services-of-the-rear and proposing that Bliss undertake to discharge political tasks. He gave as his reason a desire to free Pershing for strictly military duties, since his army had grown into a large force.[80] Pershing acquiesced in the expansion of Bliss' responsibilities, but hurriedly appointed one of his own officers, General James G. Harbord, to command the Services of Supply.[81] The decision to enlarge Bliss' responsibilities rather than to send a civilian with special powers accorded with the American desire to avoid political contacts with the Allies when possible.

Thus it came about that General Pershing suffered the loss of some of his authority. This action was a direct response to the need for enhanced inter-Allied unity. The General finally had overstepped the bounds of tolerance in Washington. His intransigence had moved the Entente Powers to conduct an ill-concealed campaign to lessen his political influence. By the time the changes made by Baker came into effect, all energies were absorbed by a powerful series of inter-Allied counteroffensives which continued until the end of hostilities.

The Administration had reached the point of insisting that inter-Allied discussions concerning the training and employment of American troops should be conducted by the permanent military representatives and that official proposals should be presented to the Supreme War Council. Late in June General March informed Bliss that "the British Ambassador has been informed that the President will not consider any project for the use of American troops [emanating] from a single nation, but that such recommendations must come from the Military Representatives at Versailles representing all the nations."[82]

When the Supreme War Council met to hold its seventh session (2-4 July), it inaugurated a series of studies to determine the scope and character of American activities in France. The British found themselves less and less able to influence the United States because the French pressed for shipping to transport American troops regardless of Pershing's plans for them.[83] Once again the need for American reinforcement strengthened the bargaining power of the United States. Whenever the French and the British failed to establish a joint policy, General Pershing could sustain his position.

After the seventh session ended, the controversy over amalgamation faded into the background. The French and British still hoped to forestall the establishment of an independent American army, clinging to their belief that it could not operate by itself until 1919, but Pershing's constant pressure brought about the formation of the First American Army in August. It conducted a limited offensive against the Saint-Mihiel salient in September and followed this initial success with the much more extensive Meuse-Argonne offensive. The American army never achieved self-sufficiency, depending on the Allies until the armistice for much of its logistical support, air cover, and artillery fire. Ironically, during operations in the period September-November 1918, some European troops came under Pershing's command. They had been amalgamated into his army. When the United States decided to adopt an expanded mobilization scheme called the "eighty-division" plan, the Entente began to relax their pressure.[84] The stream of victories after July naturally tended to bury the issue of amalgamation.

The extended quarrels over amalgamation definitely enhanced mutual suspicions and jealousies within the Western coalition, a development somewhat disguised by the later activities of the Supreme War Council. These recriminations augured ill for the peace conference.[85] Pershing, stubborn to the end, never relaxed his efforts to frustrate attempts to incorporate his troops into European formations. Only victory silenced him.[86]

The evidence clearly reveals that the American opposition to amalgamation had its roots in the early decision to train and employ an independent army on the Western Front. The dynamic intransigence of General Pershing hardened this policy beyond easy alteration. The civilian leaders of the American government were unwilling to override the opinion of the principal commander in the field despite growing awareness that his attitude profoundly irritated the Entente Powers. The concealed American distrust of Europe, present even during the period of wartime cooperation, strengthened General Pershing's hand.

Fortunately, the Supreme War Council gradually gained control of the negotiations concerning amalgamation. Insofar as the issue was ever resolved, it was due to the efforts of the Council and the military representatives. Despite a general prejudice against amalgamation, the American government finally decided to restrict Pershing's powers and to centralize the discussion of amalgamation at Versailles. This action implies that Pershing had been supported by his political superiors for so long not because the Administration absolutely opposed amalgamation but because no one wished to contradict the field commander.

To what extent did a desire to influence the peace settlement by developing a powerful independent army shape the decisions of the American government? Pershing and his staff argued this point, but it was not stressed as overtly by the civilian leadership. Of course, a powerful independent army would obviously strengthen the President's hand at the peace conference. In addition, General Pershing and his advisors supported the principle of an independent force on the ground that amalgamation was an impractical and dangerous military practice. Thus from a national point of view the United States possessed both a political and a military justification for the principle of establishing an independent army. In general, President Wilson wished to defer to his military leader in respect to technical matters, and this tendency was naturally reinforced when the military attitude coincided with his political objectives. These considerations account for his generally strong support of Pershing during most phases of the long controversy. When, however, did his support for Pershing tend to waver? It wavered at times of severe military crisis, when fear of military defeat and fear of antagonizing the European leadership outweighed his usual tendency to support his commander.

This pattern of behavior supports the conclusion that the establishment of an independent army was not an absolute political *sine qua non.* It was conceived of as highly desirable from a political as well as a military point of view, but not absolutely necessary. Other influences could alter the military policy of the American government. These influences clearly were the development of a military situation in which amalgamation became necessary and a political situation in which the desire to maintain inter-Allied unity outweighed a particular national objective. Both of these influences seemed to be relevant at points during the amalgamation conflict, especially in January and June 1918. At both times the American government wavered in its support of Pershing and tactfully sought to soften the General's intransigence. Other means of controlling the peace conference seemed to exist besides the threat of military predominance inherent in the existence of a powerful and independent army, and the President could afford to give up this bargaining point if such a policy seemed expedient and if other means of control still remained.

President Wilson was deeply suspicious of Europe and Europe's ways, and he was determined to protect and enhance his power to define the terms of peace by all possible means. Military power was one of the means by which he could achieve his goal, but it was only one of several, and given his growing moral leadership, he could afford under pressure to concede something to the Entente Powers in order to sustain political unity within the Western coalition.[87]

The improving military situation in the summer of 1918 permitted Pershing to continue his efforts to establish an independent army. If the situation had not improved, it seems reasonable to argue that his objections to amalgamation would eventually have been overridden. Apologists for the intransigence of General Pershing emphasize the fact that the war ended successfully with an independent American army operating under its own commanders in its own sector. They assume that the American offensives at the Saint-Mihiel salient and the Argonne Forest convinced the German leaders that further resistance would be futile.[88] The American army never attained self-sufficiency, and perhaps the defenders of Pershing rely on an inflated estimate of the independent capabilities of the General's force. Perhaps amalgamation might have hastened the armistice.

The controversy over amalgamation reached serious proportions not only because differences in expert military opinion developed, but also because national pride and individual personalities became engaged in the debate. If the quarrel did not militate disastrously against eventual victory, it certainly enhanced the political tension which grew rapidly in inter-Allied circles even as Germany prepared to accept defeat.

CHAPTER 6

Intervention in Russia

THE success of the Bolshevik revolution in Russia early in November 1917 posed the likelihood of a complete German victory on the Eastern Front just when the Allies faced their most desperate crisis in the west. The end of the war in Russia permitted Germany to transfer many battle-hardened veterans to France, a movement which stimulated profound alarm in Allied chanceries. In order to prevent Germany from capitalizing on the collapse of Russia, the Allies developed numerous plans for armed intervention. They believed a reconstitution of the Eastern Front by means of intervention would force Germany to retain her troops in the east, a circumstance which would lessen the force of their long-anticipated spring offensive in France.

Intervention in Russia became a divisive inter-Allied issue because it would have required the United States to alter its fundamental political and military plans. The American government had been willing to enter into military cooperation with the Western Powers because all of them accepted the primacy of the concept of victory in the west. American leaders consistently opposed plans involving a diversion of military effort from France. The desire to intervene in Russia thus posed another seriously divisive issue which threatened the unity of the Western coalition. The issue therefore came before the Supreme War Council on regular occasions during 1918.

Intervention in Russia

EARLY PROPOSALS FOR INTERVENTION

The successful Bolshevik coup engineered in November 1917 established the Communists in power in Petrograd just at the time the Supreme War Council came into existence. The Russian situation was discussed at length during the inter-Allied conference in Paris late in November. Colonel House attempted to obtain a general statement of war aims to accord with the Bolshevik peace formula, "no indemnities, no annexations," but his effort proved abortive. The French and British strongly opposed a declaration of war aims, and the conferees finally decided to authorize each government to inaugurate separate contact with the Bolsheviks. Each nation would individually indicate willingness to discuss war aims with Russia when that country possessed a stable government.[1] The Allies also considered lending support to the counterrevolutionary activities of certain Russian adventurers, especially Kaledin, who was then organizing an anti-Bolshevik force in southern Russia. House manifested little interest in such proposals.[2]

The possibility of assisting Kaledin and other "white" dissidents in order to reconstitute the Eastern Front resulted in a survey of Russian conditions by the military representatives of the Supreme War Council. On 24 December 1917 they drew up Joint Note No. 5, entitled "The Situation in Russia." It proposed that the Allies render military and moral support to national groups in Russia seeking to prevent the extension of German control over important areas of that country. The joint note called attention to the great supplies of oil and wheat available in south Russia, especially if the Bolsheviks assisted Germany in obtaining them. Throughout 1918 many observers believed the Bolshevik leaders were paid agents of Germany. If Germany managed to supply itself in Russia, the impact of the Allied blockade would decline precipitately. The representatives drew attention to the difficulty of maintaining adequate communications with interior areas of Russia.[3]

Joint Note No. 5 was never implemented by the Supreme War Council. The weakness of Kaledin and other such agitators became apparent as time passed. The episode is important because it indicates the extent of Allied interest in restoring the Eastern Front.

The initiation of Russo-German peace negotiations at Brest-Litovsk set the stage for a long series of acrimonious discussions in the West designed to arrange inter-Allied intervention in Russia. The purpose ostensibly was to reconstitute the Eastern Front. The Supreme War Council tended to become the principal center of these consultations because it had been specifically established to concert just this kind of inter-Allied activity. Other institutional methods failed to resolve the issue.[4]

During January 1918 a series of proposals urging intervention in Russia poured into Washington. Late in December the American government learned of an Anglo-French effort to interest Japan in an expedition to Siberia by way of Vladivostok.[5] On New Year's Day the British Foreign Secretary informed the Ambassador in Washington that the British War Cabinet supported intervention at Vladivostok by an inter-Allied force made up mostly of Japanese troops with token British and American representation.[6] On 8 January the French delivered the first formal request for American participation in intervention. The French wanted to send an inter-Allied force composed mostly of Japanese troops to Irkutsk, a strategic point on the Trans-Siberian Railway about fifteen hundred air miles west of Vladivostok, in order to control eastern Siberia and prevent German penetration. They also wanted to provide for the accession of dissident Russians to the force, "since the expedition is to appear as being inspired by the desire of bringing the cooperation and support of the Allies to the Russian elements in Siberia that have remained true to the cause of the Entente."[7] Secretary Lansing officially rejected this overture on 16 January, arguing that it would engender a severe anti-Western reaction in Russia due to the traditional fear of Japanese expansion.[8]

Other proposals continued to arrive. The Allied ambassadors in Russia joined on 24 January in a plea for intervention. On the same day the British proposed to appoint Japan a "mandatory" of the other Powers to occupy the Trans-Siberian Railway. Lansing rebuffed this suggestion immediately with the phraseology, "most inopportune." When the Japanese indirectly sought to determine the American attitude toward intervention, Lansing requested the Entente ambassadors to inform their governments that the United States specifically opposed a free hand for Japan in Siberia.[9]

Having failed to accomplish his end through conventional channels, Arthur Balfour, the British Foreign Secretary, attempted to enlist the cooperation of Colonel House. Writing to the President's counsellor on 30 January, Balfour suggested that Japan's participation would definitively commit that country against Germany and would lessen pressure on other areas of the Far East, presumably the Philippines and China.[10] House was unimpressed. He told President Wilson that intervention was not feasible from a military point of view, that it might arouse severe antagonism in Russia, and that Slavic elements obsessed by the "Yellow Peril" would be alienated if Japan took a leading part in the occupation of Siberia.[11] Although Balfour continued to press the Colonel, House consistently repulsed the overtures.[12]

Impressed by the barrage of Allied importunings, Secretary Lansing (at the suggestion of House) asked General Bliss to give his estimate of intervention.[13] Bliss decided not to present an independent opinion to his government. Instead, he convened a special meeting of the military representatives to discuss the issue.[14] This action precipitated a full-dress consideration of intervention in Siberia by the Versailles group.

Meeting on 18 February, the military representatives debated the question at length. General Weygand indicated French support for intervention and stressed the need to protect the large store of military goods which had accumulated at Vladivostok. This consideration continued to influence Allied thinking throughout the debate over intervention. Supplies had accumulated at Murmansk and Archangel in north Russia as well as at Vladivostok in Siberia due to the breakdown of the Russian railroads. Weygand also held that occupation of Vladivostok would prevent the Germans from establishing a submarine base there with access to the Pacific. General Sackville-West unaccountably seemed to oppose a general occupation of the Trans-Siberian Railway, but the British clearly intended to support intervention. The military representatives ultimately decided to recommend occupation of the Vladivostok area, provided Japan would give guarantees of good faith. An inter-Allied commission would accompany the expedition to exercise control.[15]

The result of this conference was Joint Note No. 16, entitled "Japanese Intervention in Siberia," which was drafted by General Bliss. The joint note called for the occupation of the Trans-Siberian Railway from Vladivostok to Harbin, a center of communications in Manchuria located approximately three hundred air miles from Vladivostok. This action might involve some undesirable political consequences, but the military advantages were more important. Japan would provide the troops for this operation after giving suitable guarantees to preserve the territorial integrity and political sovereignty of Russia. A joint Allied mission would administer the occupation, and its extension westward would be considered as circumstances changed.[16]

General Bliss' concurrence in Joint Note No. 16 went further than any previous American commitment, but the evidence is clear that he considered his limited action a concession made necessary by European pressure. He believed he had accomplished an important service by limiting intervention to the small area around Vladivostok rather than the area between Vladivostok and Irkutsk. The Allies had preferred the latter. Bliss' report to Washington indicates his state of mind:

> I think the prospect of Japanese intervention in Siberia involves possible great danger and that the resulting purely military advantage will be small. . . . I have consulted my English and French colleagues and agree with them that some chance must be taken. I believe that all of the purely military advantage that can be secured will be obtained by the occupation of Vladivostok. The danger will be minimized if no attempt is made to proceed further than Vladivostok or at the most Harbin until effect on Russian sentiment both Bolshevik and Anti Bolshevik is ascertained.[17]

In a detailed letter to Secretary Baker, Bliss further elaborated his reasons for supporting Joint Note No. 16. He pointed out that recommendations of the military representatives to the Supreme War Council had to be unanimous. "There must, therefore, be more or less yielding at times on the part of each Representative or nothing would be accomplished." In order to facilitate a compromise,

Bliss had "urged that we [the military representatives] should confine ourselves to a consideration of the purely military parts of the proposition and not concern ourselves with politico-military results." This view, he wrote, had resulted in the limitation of the operation to the Vladivostok area. Rehearsing the reasons why the Allies viewed the Russian situation with such apprehension, Bliss labored to communicate the mood engendered in Europe by the prospect of German domination in Russia:

> All of these things are a matter of anxious thought here, resulting in a feeling of almost desperation which the Government in Washington must keep in mind as the probable explanation for such propositions as the recent one of Japanese intervention in Siberia. And if this feeling of desperation should be justified, we are bound to consider whether a desperate situation may not warrant desperate remedies.[18]

Despite the General's explanations, his undertaking called up immediate and vigorous opposition in Washington. He received orders to inform his colleagues that the United States had decided to withhold approval of Joint Note No. 16 pending the outcome of diplomatic negotiations on the subject of intervention.[19] It will be recalled that President Wilson was particularly irritated with the Supreme War Council at this time because of its political activities. Unquestionably Bliss' superiors in Washington reacted strongly against the proposed joint note because of its potential political ramifications. It involved commitments which seemed most unwise to the leaders of the American government.

Predisposed to view armed action on Russian soil with distaste, the Administration was beset by confusing and contradictory advice from "experts" on Russian developments. This situation naturally encouraged procrastination. General William V. Judson, formerly the American Military Attaché in Petrograd, strongly opposed intervention, arguing that it might force Russia into open cooperation with Germany, especially if Japan took a leading part. Judson thought the "magnificent distance" of Russia would eventually discomfit the Germans, just as it had caused Napoleon's defeat in 1812.[20] On the other hand, Maddin Summers, the American Consul General in Moscow, pressed for intervention, proposing that the Allies rally nationalist elements in Russia for a stand against the Germans in the Ural Mountains.[21] Meanwhile the British and French governments continued to urge intervention.[22]

George Kennan has written compellingly of the confusion and misunderstanding which characterized Soviet-American relations in 1918. American representatives in Russia were divided among themselves. One group led by Raymond Robins, the American Red Cross representative, advocated a conciliatory policy toward the Bolsheviks. Another group, composed of diplomats and members of the American propaganda machine in Russia, hoped for the overthrow of the Soviet regime and the restoration of bourgeois control.[23] Students of intervention unanimously observe that the chaos which prevailed and the conflicting reports which emanated from Russia definitely limited the capacity of other governments to develop a workable policy.

The growing pressure upon the United States indicated that the President soon would have to make a definite statement indicating the American attitude toward intervention if he wished to maintain some influence over the course of events in Russia.

THE AMERICAN NOTE OF 5 MARCH 1918 TO JAPAN

Beset by conflicting advice and confused information,

President Wilson had moved uncertainly in developing a policy on Bolshevik Russia. In his Fourteen Points address of 8 January 1918, he had responded to Colonel House's suggestion that he indicate sympathy for Russia and its desire for peace. House hoped to keep the Bolsheviks in the war and sought to avoid antagonizing them unduly.[24] Secretary Lansing, who was much more sensitive than House to the ideological implications of the Bolshevik Revolution, advocated a policy of nonrecognition.[25] In common with many other leaders at the time, Lansing convinced himself that the Bolshevik regime was a passing phenomenon, soon destined to succumb.[26] He hoped a policy of nonrecognition would hasten the Soviet decline and would preclude diplomatic exchanges which might prove embarrassing in the future. The President's statement on Russia in his speech of 8 January represented an attempt to encourage Russian resistance against Germany. He called upon the Central Powers to evacuate Russia, and he urged the nations of the world to join in moral and material cooperation designed to establish a responsible government in Russia. "The treatment accorded Russia by her sister nations in the months to come," the President proclaimed, "will be the acid test of their good will, of their comprehension of her needs as distinguished from their own interests, and of their intelligent and unselfish sympathy." [27]

Events during January and February forced the President's hand. Early in March he decided to take action. He showed Secretary Lansing a draft note to Japan which indicated American willingness to condone limited intervention in Siberia. The expedition would prevent German infiltration.[28] President Wilson had been swayed by concerted Allied pressure and by indications that Japan would act regardless of American policy. Although the draft note sought to place severe restrictions on Japan's freedom of action, it represented a basic change in American policy.

Colonel House suddenly undertook to alter the contents of the note to Japan, although there are indications that he had approved it previously.[29] House feared above all that the President might sacrifice his status as the leading exponent of a peace of understanding and justice if he condoned intervention in Russia. The Colonel was deeply impressed by a forceful memorandum prepared by a State Department official, William C. Bullitt, which expressed the same view. Wilson, wrote Bullitt, had built up his prestige as a fair and impartial statesman to whom the peoples of the world could turn in time of need. "The President," he concluded, "must oppose invasion of Siberia in the name of democracy and liberalism. He must act, or his position as moral leader of the world will be lost."[30] During this period Elihu Root, the leading Republican expert on Russia, also urged a policy of restraint upon House, basing his attitude on the familiar view that armed action would precipitate a Russo-German fusion against the West.[31]

House argued his case powerfully in an urgent letter he sent to the President on 3 March:

> We are treading upon exceedingly delicate and dangerous ground, and are likely to lose that fine moral position you have given the Entente cause. The whole structure which you have built up so carefully may be destroyed over night, and our position will be no better than that of the Germans.
>
> I cannot understand the fatuous determination of the British and French to take such a step. Leaving out the loss of moral advantage, it is doubtful whether there will be any material gain.[32]

Thus House opposed intervention primarily because it was

fraught with political danger and secondarily because it did not promise concrete military success. American policy thereafter stemmed from these basic premises.

Under the pressure from Colonel House, the President decided to reverse his position and to revise his note to Japan. Dispatched to Tokyo on 5 March, the final message constituted a powerful rejection of intervention by the United States, although it did not attempt specifically to dictate the policy of Japan. The United States, the President began, had "utmost confidence" in Japan but was "bound in frankness to say that the wisdom of intervention seems . . . most questionable." The United States, he continued, would assume that the Japanese aim, should that government decide to intervene in Siberia, would be to prevent a German conquest. He thought the final disposition of Siberian questions should be made by the postwar peace conference. In order to justify his stand, the President included what amounted to a diplomatic paraphrase of Colonel House's letter:

> It is the judgment of the Government of the United States, uttered with the utmost respect, that, even with such assurances given [willingness to let the peace conference settle Siberian questions], they could in the same way be discredited by those whose interest it was to discredit them; that a hot resentment would be generated in Russia itself, and that the whole question might play into the hands of the enemies of Russia, and particularly of the enemies of the Russian revolution, for which the Government of the United States entertains the greatest sympathy, in spite of all the unhappiness and misfortune which for the time being has sprung out of it.[33]

The only parts of the original draft remaining in the final note were protestations of American confidence in Japan.[34]

The refusal of President Wilson to accept the initiative offered by Joint Note No. 16 stemmed logically from his attitude toward the Supreme War Council. The United States was unwilling to condone inter-Allied projects which threatened American war aims and peace plans. Intervention in Russia promised to cause a diversion of effort from the Western Front, to lessen the President's stature as leader of global liberalism, and to permit Japan to violate the principle of the open door. Perhaps the most important of these considerations was the threat to the President's ability to dominate the peace settlement.[35]

THE IMPACT OF THE GERMAN OFFENSIVE, MARCH-JUNE 1918

The note of 5 March was intended to be a definitive American pronouncement on intervention, but events conspired to keep the issue constantly before the Allies. The Treaty of Brest-Litovsk, signed on 3 March 1918, took Russia completely out of the war. By abandoning huge sections of the country to Germany, the Bolsheviks made possible a wholesale transfer of German troops to the Western Front and a concerted German effort to extort foodstuffs, oil, and other desperately needed supplies from Russia. The treaty could not fail to intensify Entente interest in intervention.[36] The great German offensive of March dramatized the adverse effects of the Russian defalcation and served to pose the question of intervention far more urgently than during the earlier months of 1918. During the military crisis which endured until July, the Allies failed to obtain American consent to intervention through conventional diplomatic channels, a circumstance which led them to present many of their proposals to the Supreme War Council.

The Treaty of Brest-Litovsk did not stimulate immediate changes in American policy. Russia retained its status as an associate of the United States, although the American government did not extend *de facto* recognition to the Bolshevik regime.[37] The Japanese delayed their reply to the President's note of 5 March for some two weeks, but they finally indicated their willingness to hold intervention in abeyance for the time being. Although they reserved freedom of action, the Japanese attitude strengthened the Americans *vis-à-vis* the Allies.[38] The United States could resist European pressure with some assurance that Japan would not act without prior consultation.[39]

The Supreme War Council took up the Russian question during its fourth session in London on 14 March. Instead of discussing the situation during formal meetings, the Council referred the subject to a special "political conference" of the Entente Powers.[40] This step was taken in deference to President Wilson's protest of February against political discussions held by the Supreme War Council. The political conference referred the Russian issues to a joint meeting of the military representatives and the naval representatives attached to the Allied Naval Council.[41] The meeting failed to produce significant recommendations.[42]

At this time the possibility of sending an expedition to north Russia in order to protect their interests in the Murmansk-Archangel area began to interest the Allies. In the future, discussions concerning Russia would consider the north Russian expedition as well as the eastern Siberian expedition. For various reasons, the United States early developed different attitudes toward the two expeditions.

During March and April the French and the British both advanced new arguments to bolster the case for intervention. The British became fearful that German penetration in Russia might threaten their holdings in south Asia, particularly Afghanistan and India.[43] A study prepared by the British Section of the Supreme War Council suggested that Germany might fan the flames of Pan-Islamism and thus encourage insurrections in the British possessions. Unlike previous British documents urging intervention, it denounced Bolshevism. "Government can only be carried on by educated people. . . . Soviets of illiterate workmen will not do." The study conceded that intervention in Russia might require territorial concessions to Japan. The writer thought this step might lessen Japanese pressure on other parts of Asia.[44] Bliss saw a copy of this document. It was a tactless piece of work, stressing colonialism, anti-Bolshevism, and territorial compensation for Japan. The United States would obviously respond unfavorably to all three appeals.

The French began to fear that Germany might recruit additional troops in Russia for use against the Allies in the west. They thought Germany might repatriate prisoners of war and rearm them, or might organize them into a powerful force capable of seizing Siberia.[45] There were large numbers of prisoners incarcerated along the Trans-Siberian Railway. The United States government tended to discount this argument after receiving reports from American observers in Russia which indicated no immediate threat of such activity.[46]

Having encountered severe opposition in Washington, the Allies turned their attention to Versailles. Early in April the British brought a draft note on the Russian question before the military representatives. Joint Note No. 20, entitled "The Situation in the Eastern Theatre," pulled together the principal arguments in support of intervention. Its major premise was that Germany would meet no serious resistance in Russia unless an immediate expedition were launched by the Allies in order to reconstitute the Eastern Front. The aims of intervention would be: to reduce the area from which Germany could draw materials and manpower, to check German penetration into south Russia and Persia, and to prevent withdrawal of German troops to France. The expedition would lend support to Russian and non-Russian elements willing to resist Germany. "In Siberia that support can only be given effectively by the Japanese, with the eventual assistance of Czech and other elements which can be organized on the spot."[47] The reference to the Czechs acknowledged the presence in Siberia of a large contingent of Czech troops which had fought with the Russians against the Central Powers. After the Treaty of Brest-Litovsk these men remained in Siberia, under arms, well disciplined, and ready for action. They were attempting to move eastward along the Trans-Siberian Railway toward Vladivostok. Almost unnoticed at this point, the "Czech Legion" was to become one of the most important elements in the Siberian situation during the summer of 1918. The note specified that the Japanese force to be used as part of the expedition would not be an army of occupation, but rather "a mobile base or nucleus of regular armed force affording moral, material, and if necessary, military support to mobile Russian detachments." The expedition would be nominally international in character.

Much to the irritation of his colleagues, General Bliss resolutely refused to sign Joint Note No. 20. He was fully aware that his government adamantly opposed intervention. He shared the dominant opinion of American military leaders that intervention in Russia would not materially strengthen the strategic position of the Allies.[48] As a strong adherent of the "western strategy," he generally opposed military adventures elsewhere than in France. Unwilling to disturb the Entente leaders unduly, the tactful Bliss torpedoed Joint Note No. 20 as painlessly as possible. Without his signature the note could not be forwarded to the Supreme War Council. He explained to the other military representatives that he could not sign the note because it dealt with matters being discussed by his government through other channels, but he agreed to transmit its contents to Washington.[49] Once again American resistance had frustrated inter-Allied efforts to arrange intervention in Russia.

The next action of the military representatives was to consider the plight of the Czech Legion. In April 1918 the force numbered approximately 50,000 men. It was proceeding slowly eastward along the Trans-Siberian Railway. The Czech movement toward Vladivostok was to be the first phase of a long journey to the Western Front by way of the Pacific, the United States, and the Atlantic. The Allies became increasingly interested in the progress of the Czechs as the prospect of American acquiescence in intervention seemed to fade away.

On 27 April the military representatives approved Joint Note No. 25, entitled "Transportation of Czech Troops from Siberia," which actually envisioned the use of the Czechs to defend Siberia against German penetration. The note proposed that the Czechs leave Russia by way of both eastern Siberia and north Russia. The concentration of Czechs at Murmansk and Vladivostok would provide troops for use in a possible intervention. Thus the note concerned itself more with the disposition of Czechs for military purposes in Russia than with their transport to France.[50]

When the Supreme War Council met at Abbeville on 1-2 May, it officially accepted Joint Note No. 25. The French particularly interested themselves in the Czechs and placed officers with them to assist their progress. Technically, these men were a part of the French army. Some effort was made to provide transportation for them, but even at this early date the Allied leaders thought in terms of utilizing them to secure Russia against German penetration rather than in terms of a huge repatriation to France.[51]

Events at Versailles had brought General Bliss to the conviction that the Russian situation was fraught with great danger for the United States. His opposition to intervention, particularly at Vladivostok, tended to stiffen perceptibly as he learned more about European motives. Cabling to Secretary Baker on 26 May, he noted the French interest in the Russian debt which the Soviets had repudiated. He thought intervention would fail unless it met with a cordial welcome on the part of the Russian people. Otherwise a German-dominated resistance against Allied encroachment might cause Japan to join with Germany in order to divide Siberia into respective spheres of influence. "We may find the East combining with Middle Europe against the West." He expressed profound skepticism about European opinions on the Russian question:

> I distrust everything I hear on this subject here. I hear only denunciation of the Bolsheviks and everything they stand for. I think most would like to see something like the old regime restored. . . . My present disposition is to consent only to a recommendation that the Allied Governments ascertain beyond shadow of doubt what the real attitude of the Russian people will be toward this intervention. . . . Can I be advised as to whether my Government desires me to continue in the attitude that the Military Representatives, having already submitted this question to their Governments, must await their decision before saying anything further? If not what general policy is it desired that I follow on this subject?[52]

General Bliss' request for instructions elicited a general statement of American policy in a message from General March on 28 May:

> The President's attitude is that Russia's misfortune imposes upon us at this time the obligation of unswerving fidelity to the principles of Russian territorial integrity and political independence. Intervention via Vladivostok is deemed impractical because of the vast distance involved, the size of the force necessary to be effective, and financing such a [project] . . . would mean a burden which the United States at this time ought not assume. . . . Such an intervening expedition would have to penetrate into European Russia. . . . Its appearance would be such that German propagandists would be able to persuade the Russian people that compensation at their expense and out of their territory was ultimately to be exacted. . . . The [idea] of compensating Japan by territory in Asiatic Russia is inadmissable.[53]

This statement, in several respects a paraphrase of the President's note to Japan of 5 March, clearly paralleled Bliss' general attitude. Secretary Lansing implemented the same policy in American diplomatic circles, sending the following cable to Ambassador William G. Sharp in Paris: "There seems to be no justification for a change in the policy of this Government." [54]

Just at this time, however, an event of great importance was transforming the situation in Siberia. The Bolsheviks earlier had manifested a cooperative attitude in helping to expedite the movement of the Czechs out of Russia by way of the north Russian ports and Vladivostok. On 25 May commenced a Czech uprising against the Bolsheviks, which resulted in the seizure by the Legion of large sections of the Trans-Siberian Railway during June.[55] The Entente leaders seized upon the Czech uprising as another justification for intervention, the French and British arguing that a strong Japanese force should come to the support of the Legion. This argument was to carry great weight with President Wilson later in the summer.

From this point on, the absolute character of American resistance to intervention began to crumble.

Already there had been indications that American policy toward intervention might change, given new conditions in Russia. The failure of the President to support intervention in eastern Siberia drew attention to the prospect of intervention in the north. The United States was somewhat receptive to intervention at Murmansk and Archangel because it seemed to promise tangible military results —there were stores to be protected there as at Vladivostok —and because Japan would not be involved. Secretary Lansing drew a sharp distinction between the two potential sites of intervention.[56] The President accepted Lansing's distinction but opposed a north Russian expedition on the familiar ground that it would divert troops from France.[57]

Under continued pressure from Britain, the President withdrew his objections to a limited operation in north Russia, and his change of front precipitated an immediate response by the Supreme War Council.[58] Bliss informed the military representatives of the American change of front on 1 June:

> The President is in sympathy with any practical military efforts which can be made at and from Murmansk and Archangel, but such efforts should proceed, if at all, upon the sure sympathy of the Russian people and should not have as their ultimate objects any restoration of the ancient regime or any other interference with the political liberty of the Russian people.[59]

The military representatives then approved Joint Note No. 31, entitled "Allied Intervention at Russian Allied Ports," which outlined a program for the occupation of north Russia. It advocated the seizure of Murmansk, followed by a similar action at Archangel. Detachments of Czechs, presumably then moving northward to Murmansk, would provide additional manpower. (Actually, no Czechs ever arrived in the north.) The Allies would send four to six battalions of infantry under the orders of a British officer who would serve as commander of the expedition.[60] The Supreme War Council officially accepted Joint Note No. 31 on 3 June, and the British hastened to launch the north Russian expedition.[61]

American willingness to sanction a limited operation in north Russia stemmed from the belief that activity there would not cause undue political embarrassments. It seemed to promise concrete military gains. After the Supreme War Council accepted Joint Note No. 31, President Wilson agreed to send a modest force to north Russia if General Foch concurred in the arrangements. The United States Navy sent a warship, the *Olympia,* to the White Sea as the vanguard of the American expedition.[62] The War Department, stubbornly continuing to oppose American activity in Russia, viewed the decisions of the President with considerable distaste and managed to delay the shipment of American troops to north Russia for the moment.[63]

The Supreme War Council also took up the question of Siberia during their meeting of 1-3 June. Seeking to provide a justification for Japanese participation in the Siberian movement, the prime ministers expressed a desire to maintain the territorial integrity of Russia and stated their confidence in the friendly intentions of Japan. They hoped the Japanese would agree to launch an expedition that would penetrate deeply into the Siberian interior, probably as far west as Cheliabinsk, just east of the Urals. They anticipated that this movement would bring the Japanese into contact with the German army. The United States remained the only obstacle to the launching of an expedition. The prime ministers finally resolved to sound out Japan as to her willingness to join in intervention on the basis previously discussed.[64] A special proposal was dispatched to Tokyo. The deliberations of the sixth session of the Supreme War Council thus prepared the ground for a formal diplomatic approach to the Japanese by the Entente Powers. The United States, of course, was not a party to this invitation. The stage was now set for the ultimate decision on intervention, which came in July.

General Bliss' suspicions of European intentions deepened during June. In a long letter to General March, he reviewed the entire course of the dispute over intervention and reiterated his belief that armed action in Russia would in the end react against the interests of the Allies. Bliss agreed with Colonel House that intervention would dangerously undermine American prestige abroad. He commented on the increasing bitterness toward the Bolsheviks in Europe. "Everyone here," he wrote, "seems imbued with a growing and bitter hatred of the Bolshevik Government and, I believe, would welcome anything that could cause its complete destruction."[65]

For his part General March reflected the dominant views of the War Department in Washington. Commenting on Bliss' letter, he stressed the extremely difficult logistical problems that would arise in connection with intervention and emphasized the likelihood that it would strengthen Germany's hand in Russia. He believed a decisive victory over Germany on the Western Front would enable the United States to dictate a settlement of the Russian situation which would satisfy all concerned.[66] The American military establishment was united in believing that intervention would be militarily impractical and politically dangerous or unnecessary.

Events fast approached a climax. Although the American opposition to intervention had subtly weakened, the Allies had no reason to expect a fundamental change in the President's attitude. Early in July the Supreme War Council forced a partial resolution of the Russian question; it presented the United States with the most powerful and urgent plea for intervention yet propounded by the Allies.

THE AMERICAN ACCEPTANCE OF LIMITED INTERVENTION, JULY 1918

Gathering on 2 July for its seventh session, the Supreme War Council immediately took up the Russian situation. Japan had responded to the contact which stemmed from the action of the Supreme War Council in June. The Japanese agreed to intervene at Vladivostok, provided the United States concurred in the move. They wished to proceed only as far as Irkutsk, about half the distance from Vladivostok to Cheliabinsk. The latter point had been specified in the Entente proposal.[67]

Unable to take action on the Japanese expedition without American consent, the Supreme War Council prepared a comprehensive memorandum to gain the support of President Wilson. Signed by the prime ministers of Britain, France, and Italy, it was forwarded immediately to Washington. Realizing that the plight of the Czech Legion had evoked widespread sympathy and interest in the United States, the prime ministers argued that the presence of the Czechs in Siberia would lessen internal opposition to the proposed expedition. Stressing their belief that Bolshevism was in decline, they argued that intervention in Siberia would strengthen the hand of "liberal" factions within Russia who desired Allied action.

The prime ministers dwelt on the significance of Japan's willingness to respect the territorial integrity and political independence of Russia. The Japanese attitude, they argued, cleared the way for immediate action to relieve pressure on the Western Front. Intervention would force Germany to transfer a large body of troops to the east. If the Allies failed to intervene, the consequences would be the abandonment of the Russian people, the end of the Allied blockade on Germany, and the prolongation of the war.

Estimating that 100,000 troops would be required to insure success, the prime ministers noted that Japan would have to supply most of the manpower. Expeditions would have to land both at Vladivostok in Siberia and at Murmansk and Archangel in north Russia. The United States was asked to send a relief commission to organize the devastated Siberian economy. The memorandum pointed out that General Foch and the military representatives unanimously supported the plan. The message ended with a powerful plea for American support.[68]

Before concluding their deliberations, the prime ministers took further action to implement Joint Note No. 31, which dealt with intervention in north Russia.[69] Late in June the British had landed a small force at Murmansk. This *fait accompli* prompted General Bliss to request the dispatch of three American battalions to the north in accord with the provisions of Joint Note No. 31.[70] This action reflected the American tendency to support action in north Russia more willingly than in Siberia.

The action of the Supreme War Council clearly required a definitive restatement of American policy. The British movement at Murmansk, the support given intervention by General Foch, the activities of the Czechs, and the approach to Japan had finally forced the President's hand.

The Supreme War Council's proposal met with mixed reactions in Washington. The War Department, fixed in its opinion that intervention was impractical, continued its unqualified opposition.[71] The State Department, supported by Colonel House, was noticeably impressed by the developments of June and thenceforth tended to favor some form of intervention.[72]

President Wilson had consistently attempted to prevent action by the Allies which would lead to armed intervention in Russia, but the powerful pressure exerted through the Supreme War Council in the memorandum of 2 July convinced him that his policy of complete opposition had become obsolete. Unwilling to condone intervention but fearful of seriously alienating the Entente Powers, he decided to permit American participation in severely restricted expeditions to eastern Siberia and north Russia. His actions in the wake of the message from Versailles reflected his intense desire to limit the scope and significance of intervention, since it could no longer be completely blocked by the United States. He would insure that intervention did not cause the political embarrassment which originally had prejudiced him so powerfully against the project. In short, President Wilson hoped to maintain his own policy while seeming to accept the Entente proposal.

On 6 July the President convened a council to discuss a new Russian policy. Present were Secretaries Lansing, Baker, and Daniels, along with General March and Admiral Benson. Despite the vigorous opposition of General March, who forcefully presented the objections of the War Department, the President announced his intention to support a strictly limited intervention in Siberia.[73] The plan he outlined contemplated a joint Japanese and American expeditionary force composed of about seven thousand troops from each country. It would guard the military stores at Vladivostok and help the Czechs assemble at ports of embarkation for their voyage to France. The United States would mature plans for a relief commission to supervise the economic reconstruction of Siberia. When the expedition landed, the Allies would publish a self-denying ordinance declaring their intention to respect Russia's territorial integrity and political sovereignty. No further actions were contemplated until changing conditions warranted them.[74]

The President obviously sought to give the appearance of making measurable concessions without, in fact, allowing the Associates to undertake a large-scale invasion of Russia. His program would minimize the chance of political embarrassments and inhibit Japanese efforts to control eastern Siberia. He hoped to gain his old ends by new means. By limiting the expedition's mission at Vladivostok to the protection of the war material which had accumulated there, along with aid to the Czechs and economic assistance to Siberia, he hoped to deflate German accusations of aggression.[75] Despite continued opposition from the War Department, the President pressed his project to fruition.[76]

Secretary Lansing received instructions to make preliminary arrangements with the Japanese through their Ambassador in Washington, Count Ishii, thus eliminating the French and the British from the negotiations. The Japanese were initially receptive to the American proposals but soon manifested unwillingness to limit their forces to seven thousand men.[77] Lord Reading was furious because Britain had been shut out of the preliminaries and because the American plan did not contemplate British participation in the expedition to Vladivostok. Despite Reading's irritation, Lansing refused to include him in his conversations with Count Ishii.[78] American attempts to limit the Japanese force to seven thousand men ended in failure, and the President had to agree to the appointment of a Japanese general to command at Vladivostok.

On 17 July the President issued a definitive *aide-*

mémoire announcing American policy on secondary theaters in general and on Russia in particular. Superficially friendly in tone, the statement expressed American distrust of intervention in unmistakable terms. The President himself composed the document, although it was issued over the signature of the Secretary of State.[79]

The *aide-mémoire* began with a restatement of America's fundamental strategy, the concept of concentration on the Western Front. The United States had no selfish ends and wished to cooperate fully in the struggle against Germany, but the American government opposed extensive intervention in Russia. Such action would enhance the current political chaos there without contributing materially to the defeat of Germany. The United States could not agree to participate in a massive invasion of Russia, could not "take part in such intervention or sanction it in principle." The only justifiable aims of inter-Allied activity in Russia would be to assist the Czech Legion and to help the nation establish a stable government. Consequently the United States could agree only to an operation at Murmansk designed to safeguard the military stores accumulated there and another expedition to relieve the Czechs at Vladivostok. If these "modest and experimental" plans were to be implemented, the Allies must join the United States and Japan in giving the most solemn assurances to Russia and the world that the expeditions would strictly refrain from interference with the political sovereignty, internal affairs, and territorial integrity of Russia. A brief outline of the joint Japanese and American plans for operations at Vladivostok followed the general statement of principle. An announcement that an American commission would be sent to the Far East in order to organize the economy of Siberia concluded the list of substantive actions.

In order to soften the vaguely insulting implications

of the *aide-mémoire*, the President went out of his way to stress that he did not intend to inhibit independent actions contemplated by the Allies or Japan:

> None of the conclusions here stated is meant to bear the least color of criticism. . . . All that is intended is a perfectly frank and definite statement of policy which the United States feels obliged to adopt for herself and in the use of her military forces. . . . [The United States does not wish] to set limits to the action or define the policies of its associates.[80]

Despite this pious protestation, it is difficult to escape the conclusion that the *aide-mémoire* was intended to accomplish the very purposes it professed to renounce. Intervention on a broad scale was impossible without American support. The *aide-mémoire* specifically or inferentially refuted all the arguments advanced by the prime ministers in their message to the President. The document was a firm and unmistakable rebuff to the Entente and the Supreme War Council. It could not fail to elicit a cold response. The President had withdrawn what he had seemed to offer—all in one motion. He continued to pursue his own ends while bending slightly in the face of powerful pressure from abroad.

The British sent a reply to the *aide-mémoire* on 30 July. Approving the American plan to provide assistance for the Czechs and the Siberians, the British still thought the program highly inadequate. The message attempted to correct what the British government conceived to be two mistaken impressions. Britain had urged intervention primarily to ease the pressure on the Western Front; it did not consider the Russian expeditions to be violations of the strategy of concentration in France. Moreover, Britain also wished to act in the best interests of Russia, contrary to the implication in the *aide-mémoire*. "We wish [Russia] . . . to choose her own form of government and pursue in her own way her own line of self-development." Intervention would assist these processes.[81] Clearly the President had drawn blood.

Following the issuance of the *aide-mémoire*, the contents of which did not become publicly known until 4 August, the Supreme War Council exercised little or no influence over the course of intervention in Russia. The military representatives continued to study the situation, but the Council, which did not meet again until late in October, took no other official actions. The attempt of the Allies to utilize the Supreme War Council as the center of their efforts to alter American policy toward Soviet Russia did result in limited expeditions to north Russia and to Vladivostok, but the broad intervention contemplated in London and Paris never gained official sanction in Washington. The Japanese violated the spirit of their arrangement with the United States by greatly extending the size and strength of their forces in Siberia. General William S. Graves, the commanding general of the American troops sent to Vladivostok in August and September, continually frustrated efforts by France, Britain, and Japan to enlarge the scope of intervention. The ill-starred expedition to north Russia, like the group at Vladivostok, was withdrawn after failing to achieve its purposes.

The United States consistently followed a noninterventionist policy toward Bolshevik Russia despite powerful pressures emanating from her European associates and Japan. The Entente hoped to reconstitute the Eastern Front by means of intervention. They also hoped to hasten the demise of Bolshevism. American policy stemmed from a desire to maintain the principle of concentration in

France, a belief that intervention would not succeed, a fear that Japan would seize the opportunity to occupy huge portions of Siberia, and a fixed intention to avoid diplomatic entanglements which might lessen the President's ability to negotiate a peace of justice and reconciliation.

The Entente turned more and more to the Supreme War Council, hoping to obtain American consent to intervention through inter-Allied channels. The United States proved just as unresponsive to appeals from the Supreme War Council as it had been to pressure exerted through more conventional diplomatic channels. General Bliss was more sensitive to Allied requests than his superiors in Washington, but he shared the general American distrust of European motives as well as the conviction that the United States should not jettison the strategy of concentration on the Western Front. His instructions from Washington, even when they acquiesced in Allied desires, never varied from a tone of studied opposition to a powerful intervention in Russia.

President Wilson's policy, in common with his approach to most other political-military issues which came to his attention during World War I, reflected his single-minded determination to retain diplomatic independence. He firmly believed that only by pursuing an independent course could he arrange a peace in accord with American interests and aspirations.

The ultimate American decision to participate in limited expeditions to Siberia and north Russia represented an attempt to restrict the scope of undesirable but unavoidable inter-Allied adventures.[82] The decision stemmed from a desire to discourage untoward incursions on Russian sovereignty, although the American government steadily grew in knowledge of, and opposition to, the principles espoused by Bolshevik Russia. In this case, as in most others, the

United States specifically sought to separate political from military considerations in its dealings with the Supreme War Council, hoping to avoid entangling political commitments.

CHAPTER 7

The Supreme War Council and the Macedonian Campaign

WHEN the German attacks in France began to decline in strength during the summer of 1918, interest in other theaters began to increase perceptibly. Russia certainly attracted the greatest attention, but the Allies had other areas in mind as well. France had become closely identified with the campaign against Bulgaria being conducted in Macedonia, and Britain hoped to enlarge its military effort against Turkey in Palestine and Mesopotamia. Although no one as yet believed that Germany could be brought to terms in 1918, everyone seems to have recognized that Hindenburg could no longer expect to achieve a decision in France. The qualified optimism engendered by these opinions led the French and the British to contemplate increased efforts against the Central Powers elsewhere than on the Western Front.

Some observers continued to manifest a fear of German power despite their realization that victory at last seemed almost assured. Colonel House was one of these. Writing to the President late in June, he commented on current needs and speculated on the future:

> England, France and Italy need now constant stimulation and no one can do it so well as you. If their morale can be kept up to Autumn in my opinion, our fight against Germany will be largely won. I believe Austria is already

> at the breaking point and I also believe the German people will take the supreme power from the military extremists this Autumn if they do not have a decisive victory on the Western Front.[1]

The American leaders, scenting victory in France if the military effort there could be sustained, naturally opposed projects which would divert men and materials from the Western Front to other areas like Macedonia and Palestine, particularly when they suspected the Allies of pursuing imperial designs. American energy centered on the immediate task of restoring the position in France and preparing a decisive counterthrust, which they hoped would bring victory in 1919. Events of the summer stimulated American suspicion of ultimate Allied intentions, especially after the disputes over amalgamation and intervention.[2]

During the period from July to October 1918, General Bliss became increasingly sensitive to European interest in military operations which seemed to him intended primarily to accomplish the political designs of the Allies and which had little relation to the task of defeating Germany on the Western Front. The French concentration on the Macedonian campaign and the British preoccupation with the Middle East particularly caught his attention. Thoroughly cognizant of his government's intense desire to avoid embarrassing political entanglements which seemed to have no connection with American war aims and peace plans, he vigorously pursued a policy of discouraging American involvement in these theaters. He sought to forestall a change in inter-Allied strategy which might shift the emphasis from Europe to the eastern theaters.

THE CONTROVERSY OVER THE SALONIKA EXPEDITION, JULY 1918

Late in 1915 the Allies had realized that Bulgaria was about to enter the war on the side of the Central Powers.

In order to sustain their influence in southeastern Europe, they landed an expeditionary force at the strategically located port of Salonika in Macedonia. The opposition of the pro-German King of Greece, Constantine, embarrassed Allied attempts to frustrate Bulgarian conquests in Macedonia and Albania. Continued difficulties in Macedonia soon discouraged the British, who wished either to withdraw from the theater or to confine their involvement to an armed camp at Salonika. They hoped to transfer the garrison from there to the Western Front, but the French insisted on holding the position.[3] The French government hoped to exploit the area after the war ended. A withdrawal of the garrison at Salonika would have been a severe blow to their postwar intentions in the Balkans.

In 1917 the Allies managed to secure the abdication of the pro-German Constantine and the establishment of a pro-Allied regime under the patriot Venizelos. He immediately declared war on the Central Powers. During the early months of 1918 the French reorganized and enlarged the Salonika garrison. By midsummer it included some twenty-nine divisions. At this point General Franchet d'Espérey replaced General Guillamat as commander of the force. The French then began to urge a powerful offensive based on Salonika designed to put Bulgaria out of the war and to threaten the southeastern flank of the Central Powers.

On 23 June 1918 Clemenceau ordered D'Espérey to plan an offensive for the autumn of 1918. A breakthrough in Macedonia would give the Greeks and the Serbians a chance to reclaim lost territories from the Bulgarians.[4] This action caused a complicated discussion of projected operations in Macedonia during the seventh session of the Supreme War Council early in July.

The Council already had concerned itself with the French activity in Macedonia. During May two generals were sent to confer with Guillamat about future activities in the theater. Guillamat strongly opposed evacuation of Salonika, maintaining that it could be held without difficulty and that its abandonment would have an adverse effect on the morale of the Greek and Serbian armies. The Serbs had been grouped at Salonika after an earlier defeat.[5] The British Section at Versailles objected strongly to expansion of the operations at Salonika. General Sackville-West, the British military representative, advocated a general withdrawal to more southerly positions in "Old Greece" in order to minimize logistical problems and to strengthen the British case for transferring troops from Salonika to other theaters.[6]

Highly irritated by what they deemed a unilateral French effort to expand the scope of the Macedonian campaign without inter-Allied consultation, the British decided to bring up the issue during the seventh session of the Supreme War Council. The revealing diary of General Sir Henry Wilson indicates that the British seriously interested themselves in an expansion of their operations against the Turks in Palestine:

> A long discussion this morning [3 July] as to what we are to say to the French about Versailles and Salonika. I remain of the opinion that I expressed at the time of the Doullens and Beauvais Agreements, that when we handed our army over to Foch, we should announce that we took over all the salt water and all theatres over the salt water except France and Italy. Neither Lloyd George nor Milner agree with me. I pointed out that I should probably want 4 or 5 divisions from France for Palestine, and that we ought now to make this clear to the French. But, although Lloyd George quite agreed, and [they] were all in favour of my going on with preparations, they were against saying anything about them to the French. This is quite wrong. Lloyd George agreed to take up the question of

Salonika and Foch's and Clemenceau's orders for an offensive there.[7]

When the Council convened, Lloyd George posed the question of Salonika. Clemenceau said that a previous decision to withdraw troops from the theater for use on the Western Front ought to be reconsidered because the American reinforcement had redressed the balance in France. Lloyd George then objected to the French practice of appointing commanders at Salonika without consulting the other Allies. Sir Henry Wilson presented a brief designed to show that the attempt to mount an offensive in Macedonia contradicted the strategy for the theater adopted early in 1918 by the Supreme War Council. This statement posed the issue of the future development of the Macedonian campaign quite directly. Arthur Balfour concluded the day's discussion with a significant observation. He "wished to place on record that this was not a military question only. It was also an important diplomatic question, and he would ask [the French and Italian Foreign Ministers] to consider it carefully before their next meeting."[8]

The next day the British obtained acceptance of a series of resolutions designed to preclude an extensive operation in Macedonia. The military representatives were ordered to report on the feasibility of an offensive; no action was to be taken until the report was presented; and inter-Allied consultation would precede future appointments of commanders for the force at Salonika.[9] These resolutions at least dimly suggested that the strategic design might be revised in the future if certain changes in the situation occurred. They represented a weakening of the general defensive concept which had previously governed operations in Macedonia. Neverthless, the British clearly considered their efforts at this session to have been a direct attempt to curb French ambitions in general and the Salonika build-up in particular.[10]

The dispute over Salonika was one result of British irritation with the restrictions imposed upon them by Foch's command. They hoped to restore some of the prestige the Council lost when Foch became Allied commander-in-chief. Field Marshal Haig noted Lloyd George's temper after meeting him at Versailles on 2 July: "I found [Lloyd George] very angry with the French because they were taking too large a share in the direction of the war, and gave little credit to Great Britain for what she was doing."[11]

On the final day of the seventh session, 4 July, Lloyd George presented a resolution which enhanced the authority of the military representatives and restricted the powers of Foch. In the haste of the proceedings, Clemenceau accepted the resolution, which had been drafted in English and presented hurriedly.[12] Foch immediately denounced this effort to limit French power and threatened to resign unless the Council modified its action.[13] After additional negotiations between the prime ministers, the resolution was amended to meet Foch's objections.[14] The powers of the military representatives were redefined and somewhat strengthened. General Foch retained authority over the Western Front, but his power to control other theaters was clearly restricted in scope.[15]

This action seems to have mollified the feelings of both the French and the British. Nevertheless, the Supreme War Council did not sit again until late in October, a lapse of some four months, although the Rapallo Agreement had specified regular monthly gatherings. The reasons for this hiatus are complicated, but certainly the French feared that the Council might interfere with Foch's command in order to further the interests of Britain. One way to head off this development was to avoid formal gatherings of the Council.

Of course, the swift pace of events during the summer and autumn of 1918 left little time for formal meetings of heads of government.

Although General Bliss had noted the development of the Anglo-French rivalry, specifically in connection with Macedonia, he had not intruded in the discussions. His instructions of 1 July from Secretary Baker charted his course:

> Our Government has no interest in this subject [Macedonia]. Our troops, of course, could not participate [since the United States was not at war with Bulgaria] and no action should be taken predicated upon action to be taken by the United States, nor should the Military Representatives undertake to advise the United States about its relations in this matter, but any proposed action to be carried on by the European Allies will not embarrass this Government.[16]

Baker's willingness to condone activities desired by the Entente which did not require American participation indirectly strengthened the British. On 9 July Bliss received a report from four members of his Section recommending the maintenance of a defensive stance in the Balkans. His officers argued that no gains of significance could be made even if an offensive in Macedonia succeeded in detaching the Bulgarians from the Central Powers.[17] On the same day Bliss informed his fellow military representatives of American policy as announced by Secretary Baker.[18] This view of Macedonian affairs paralleled that of the British Section.

The events of the seventh session strengthened Bliss' suspicions of French intentions in the Balkans. He thought enough of the matter to explore it at length in one of his letters to Baker. He attributed British opposition to offensive action in Macedonia to political considerations. Bliss himself tended to favor an offensive were it not for these political matters. Noting the persistent rumors that the United States might be called upon to settle the Balkan controversy, he indicated that pressure for American intervention at Salonika might develop soon. Bliss usually opposed such operations because they diverted men and materials from France. He believed the French wanted to expand their power in Greece in order to insure postwar dominance in the Balkans. The British, he thought, showed reluctance to support French aspirations because a campaign based on Salonika would be of no particular benefit to them. The Italians had fought a campaign to the west of the Salonika positions, seeking to insure control of Dalmatia at the end of hostilities. "In short," the General concluded, "the practical result of what has been done is to insure, as far as possible, at the end of the war, the retention of Salonika by the French and of Valona and the control of the Albanian coast by the Italians." [19]

Thus Great Britain and the United States had developed and expressed negative attitudes toward the Salonika campaign because it seemed to strengthen the French without offering rewards to the other members of the Western coalition. The British interested themselves in expanding their operations against Turkey in Palestine, a strategy in accord with their postwar political ambitions. The United States continued to adhere to the western strategy as the best way to force a German capitulation at the earliest possible date. This policy was in accord with American plans for the future.

DIPLOMATIC AIMS AND STRATEGY, AUGUST-OCTOBER 1918

The question of Macedonia continued to claim the attention of the military representatives, despite Anglo-

American efforts to avoid it. Late in July they discussed plans for an offensive against Bulgaria based on Salonika. General Bliss took the opportunity to reiterate the attitude of the United States, although he indicated willingness to assist in planning the operation if conditions seemed to suggest its need. Bliss thought the campaign was promising from a strictly military point of view, and he did not wish to interfere with Entente efforts to study the subject.[20] It is likely that Bliss sought to placate the French by indicating sympathy for their attitude without actually intending to strengthen the likelihood of an offensive in Macedonia.

A few days later the military representatives approved a plan for a possible Balkan offensive to take place by October 1918. General Bliss managed to insert a proviso into the resolution which revealed his actual position on the campaign:

> It is necessary to push on with all speed the preparations for an offensive in Macedonia . . . (provided that these preparations do not require any assistance in men or material from the Western Front, and do not divert any tonnage, now or subsequently available, which is required for the continuous arrival at the maximum rate of reinforcements in effectives and material indispensable to the execution of the plan for the Western Front approved by [Foch]).

General Sackville-West concurred in this action, presumably because he thought the campaign would never materialize. Acceptance of the plan would strengthen morale in Greece and respect the desires of Foch. The British authorized the plan simply because they did not think it would ever be used. Once again American policy reflected a desire to avoid commitments in secondary theaters which might weaken the effort in France.[21]

The expectations of Bliss and Sackville-West proved inaccurate. The French transcended the limiting intentions of the military representatives simply by ignoring them. General Guillamat, still active in the effort to launch an offensive in Macedonia despite his removal from command, obtained British and Italian consent to a projected campaign from Salonika by means of personal representations in London and Rome.[22] The energetic preparations of D'Espérey accomplished the rest.[23] The smashing success of the offensive late in September succeeded in detaching Bulgaria from the Central Powers and contributed materially to the German decision to seek an armistice.[24]

General Bliss especially welcomed the *aide-mémoire* of 17 July which announced American policy on intervention in Russia. It provided a general policy for dealing with Allied efforts to launch campaigns in secondary theaters.[25] Early in August Bliss expressed his views clearly in a letter to General March:

> [The *aide-mémoire*] . . . announcing the policy of our Government as to the use of American troops in Europe and making the Western Front in France our principal field of military effort, has remarkably cleared the air here. It has enabled me to head off more than one effort to commit us to other fields where I believe our tonnage and materials and men would be wasted. I have taken the ground that our troops, coming and to come, are reinforcements for the Western Front and that, therefore, any suggested plan which contemplates removing any part of them to some other front must be approved by General Foch before I will give it consideration. I know what General Foch's views are and am sure that he will not permit any diversion of our effort unless there be a compelling necessity for it.[26]

In August the military representatives undertook to prepare a detailed recommendation suggesting grand strategy for the rest of 1918 and for 1919. Bliss communicated his views on strategy to the War Department, apparently to elicit approval. He thought a victory in France would cause the general collapse of the Central Powers. Therefore the Allies should concentrate on achieving a decision on the Western Front. To this end the Allies needed a numerical superiority of a million men in rifle strength, assuming that German morale and logistical capabilities remained at their present levels. The United States would supply troops to make up for losses sustained by the Allies. The United States should oppose diversion of American troops and materials to secondary theaters and should insist on maintaining the primacy of the western strategy. He called for a limited offensive in France during the rest of 1918 in order to prepare for the final campaign in 1919. A defensive strategy was recommended for Italy, Macedonia, Palestine, and Mesopotamia.[27]

Bliss' recommendations reflected his growing belief that the Allies had become preoccupied with the task of consolidating their positions in certain secondary theaters in order to strengthen their political prospects in the post-war era. He lost no time communicating these suspicions to Secretary Baker:

> I believe the United States should aim at a successful termination of the war in 1919, and should make that the paramount question and in all of its dealings with the Allies should keep that question to the front. . . . They [the Entente Governments] agree that it [the war] can be ended only by American troops, supplies, and money. But I can see it in every discussion at which I am present, and in nearly every paper that is submitted to me, that when the end comes they want certain favorable military conditions to have been created in different parts of the world that will warrant demands to be made of the United States which they think will be, perhaps, the principal

> arbiter of peace terms. If these sufficiently favorable military situations are not created on certain secondary theatres by the beginning of the Autumn of next year our Allies may be willing to continue through 1920, *at the cost of United States troops and money*, a war which may be ended with complete success, as far as we are concerned, by operations on the Western Front in 1919.[28]

Bliss then suggested a definite attempt to commit the Allies to a program designed to end the war in the next year. He thought Foch should be approached and asked to state his estimate of the military effort required to defeat Germany in 1919. This estimate could then be used to create an overwhelming public opinion in favor of an early end to the war. European intrigues could thus be frustrated. Bliss summarized his motives in a final comment: "Is it not worthwhile to save the blood and treasure that must be spent in 1920 if we can, by any possibility, end the war in 1919?"

The American military representative doggedly continued to advocate his plan. In another message to Baker and March, he reiterated his previous proposal and held that the United States should force the issue at the next session of the Supreme War Council if General Foch refused to make recommendations.[29] Later in the month he reported that Foch had given an estimate of the effort required to achieve victory in 1919. French and British formations would have to be maintained at full strength, and the Americans would have to place a hundred divisions in France for the ensuing campaign.[30] Henceforth Bliss strongly supported the so-called "hundred-division plan." The War Department finally concurred in an "eighty-division plan."[31]

The unsettled nature of the times was mirrored in Bliss' suspicion that the Entente might accept an unsatisfactory peace settlement during the latter months of 1918. He thought public opinion in Europe might force the leaders to conclude a peace which would postpone rather than settle the issues which divided the belligerents. Bliss wanted to commit the Allies to a definite program for 1919 in order to head off unsound operations in secondary theaters and also a premature end to hostilities. Writing to Baker, Bliss continued to express his suspicions concretely:

> In our work here political questions are, as yet somewhat vaguely but more and more persistently, pushing themselves to the front, and I have a hard time steering the American Section clear of them. It cannot be denied that in certain of the campaigns in which our Allies are deeply interested, world-politics play an important part. . . . What people here are now interested in is getting the United States involved in these political questions for the purpose of enabling them better to shape their military campaigns. For their purpose, they want certain questions settled before peace comes, not after. . . . What concerns some of the Allies is not so much a political agreement, as being a necessary basis for sound military strategy, as it is a pure and simple political agreement which they think can be arrived at only under enemy pressure and before the final victory.[32]

Bliss also noted a British attempt to establish a board of political representatives as advisors to the Supreme War Council, organized along the lines of the board of military representatives, in order to draw up a general diplomatic program for the Allies. The United States had consistently opposed just this kind of political activity by the Council.[33]

Colonel House also reacted to the increasing preoccupation of the Entente with postwar politics. Writing to President Wilson early in September, he suggested that the United States ought to commit the Allies to some of the principles for which American soldiers were fighting in

France. In support of this suggestion he composed an eloquent forecast of the future:

> As the Allies succeed, your influence will diminish. This is inevitable. By the time of the Peace Conference you will be nearing the end of your second term and this, too, will be something of a challenge to those, both at home and abroad, who have the will to oppose you. Therefore, I believe you should commit the Allies now to as much of your program as is possible. It is not probable that the personnel of the allied governments will be changed if things continue to go well, and you should count upon having to reckon with Lloyd George, Clemenceau, Sonnino and their kind. This would mean a hostile rather than a sympathetic membership.
>
> Could not a plan be brought out by which the Entente would be committed to certain things for which we stand and [which] are so essential, from our point of view, to the reconstruction of the world [?]
>
> If the group I have mentioned come to the Congress flushed with victory, no appeal that you can make over their heads will be successful. In each country there will be men of vision and loftiness of purpose who will rally to your support, but they will be in the minority and their voices will be heard faintly by the great exultant throng intoxicated not alone by victory but by the thought of freedom from war.[34]

Thus both military and political leaders of the United States had become alarmed by the Allied efforts to arrange a postwar settlement distinctly at variance with American aspirations. The American military establishment wanted a strategy designed to forestall diversionary campaigns; the American statesmen wanted a policy designed to prevent unfortunate political consequences. The developments of 1918 heightened the mood of distrust which had influenced American relations with the Entente Powers throughout the war. There were distinct indications that the President would be forced to assume an activist role in the struggle to control the peace settlement.

New activities on the part of the British seemed to validate the correctness of the House-Bliss interpretation of Allied intentions. The President was particularly irritated when Lloyd George issued a statement in September implying that Britain would condone the destruction of Germany's international trade after the war. Since President Wilson's careful effort to encourage dissension in the Central Powers depended on enemy awareness of the just and humane purposes of the Western Powers and the United States, harsh statements of war aims by the British, French, and Italians met with sharp expressions of American disapproval.[35]

The President was infuriated when Washington began to suspect Britain of trying to insure postwar domination of world markets to the detriment of the United States and other countries.[36] His rancor is reflected in his comment to Edward N. Hurley, Chairman of the Shipping Board, regarding British efforts to strengthen their position in international markets:

> It is past hoping that they [the British] should believe us to be fair and square. . . . Therefore is it not best to say nothing about it? My object is to give them not even the slightest of provocation or excuse for what they are doing.[37]

Portents of devious Allied doings thus filtered to President Wilson through several channels. These various indications, combined with traditional American distrust of European motives, tended more and more to worry American leaders. None was more deeply disturbed than the President himself.

On 10 September the military representatives approved Joint Note No. 37, entitled "Military Policy of the Allies for the Autumn of 1918 and for the Year 1919." A glance at its text shows that it represented a victory for General Bliss. It advocated the western strategy with unmistakable clarity:

> France and Italy remain, as always, the main theatres of the war. . . .
> The Allies must, therefore, concentrate their resources both in manpower and material on the Western Front for the decisive struggle.
> The decisive defeat of the enemy coalition can only be achieved on the portion of the Western Front between the North Sea and Switzerland. . . .
> The defeat of the Central Powers in any of the subsidiary theatres of war could only be a step on the road to the defeat of Germany; it could not bring about the final decision.[38]

The long tenure of General Bliss and the increasing size of the United States army strengthened the prestige of the American military representative at Versailles. He managed to restrict the scope of recommendations in Joint Note No. 37 having to do with Palestine, Mesopotamia, and Russia. The note merely reiterated the earlier decision on Macedonia, repeating the proviso against diversion of men and materials to that theater from the Western Front.

The events of the summer had strengthened General Bliss' natural distrust of European motives, but they had also deepened his understanding of the purposes which could be served by the Supreme War Council.[39] When he first arrived in Versailles, he had been firm in his belief that the United States should be concerned strictly with the military aspects of the campaign in France. Writing to Colonel House in September 1918, he expressed a more expansive view:

> I am now convinced that the true function of the Su-

> preme War Council is the determination of questions of general [military] policy upon which all of the Allies can agree. And these questions relate to other fronts than the one in France. It is true that the United States has no special interest in what is happening on some of these other fronts because what is being done is not so much for the purpose of helping to bring the war to a speedy conclusion by our victory over the Germans so much as it is to carry out certain matters of national policies which were dormant before the war and which the war has brought into active life because of the opportunity which the respective nations think it gives for their realization. Nevertheless, the United States does have an interest in some of these activities in the subsidiary theatres because the greater the effort which our Allies make there the greater is the effort which the United States will be required to make here on the Western Front which is the decisive one.[40]

Unlike some of his superiors in Washington, Bliss was now aware that nations in coalition could not afford to ignore each other's ambitions and purposes.

After further thought, Bliss sought Secretary Baker's approval of a general statement of American attitudes to be communicated to the other military representatives. He hoped by this action to resist increasing pressure being brought to bear upon him to support military operations not in accord with American purposes. His draft statement began with the observation that since the United States was not formally allied with the Entente Powers, the majority could not properly expect to determine American policy: "Our Government has carefully avoided such an alliance, for the very purpose of retaining its right to individual judgment." The United States, he thought, should concentrate on victory in France and resist the "additional ulterior objects" of the Allies which might result in diverting American power to subsidiary theaters. "The United

States says to them plainly that they can do this without any objection from it, but they must not expect it or demand it to accompany them."[41] Normally quite circumspect in dealing with his colleagues at Versailles, Bliss was now willing to speak rather bluntly in order to insure victory in 1919.

The prospect of victory in 1918 had not yet seriously entered Bliss' mind. In this nearsightedness he was joined by almost every leader of the coalition against the Central Powers. By October 1918 Bliss conceived of his function in Versailles primarily as a bastion against European efforts to divert military power from France to other theaters.

THE FIVE PARTICULARS, SEPTEMBER 1918

The various pressures tending to force President Wilson's hand—all of which enhanced American suspicions of Allied motives—were crystallized by the first peace note to emanate from the Central Powers. On 16 September the Swedish Legation in Washington forwarded a note from Austria-Hungary to the White House. It called for confidential negotiations between the belligerents in order to develop general principles for a peace settlement. The decisions made by the negotiators were to be confidential, and the participants were to avoid public pronouncements "intended to thrill the masses."[42] Having reached the last extremities of exhaustion, the Austrians turned to President Wilson because his vision of the postwar settlement seemed to be their best hope for the future.

The Austrian action heightened a new mood of anticipation which had begun to develop in Europe. Rapidly recovering from the despondency which had prevailed in many places, the Allied leaders tended to stiffen in the face of the prospect that President Wilson might bargain away the fruits of victory.[43] For the first time the thought of victory in 1918 began to gain currency. The success of the offensives being conducted by Marshal Foch encouraged this note of optimism. The very quickness of victory caught the Entente unprepared for the negotiations between President Wilson and the Central Powers which ensued in October.

The President immediately rejected the Austrian peace feeler, saying that it proposed to discuss issues on which the United States had already expressed unalterable opinions.[44] The Allies unanimously thought that the Austrian note was a transparent effort to create dissension within the Western coalition.[45] This general agreement concealed serious antagonisms, which surged closer to the surface with each new indication that the Central Powers intended to sue for peace.[46]

Hoping to counteract European maneuvers for a peace on the Carthaginian model, the President decided to comment once again on American war aims. Speaking on 27 September in New York City, he announced the Five Particulars. Impartial justice, he thought, should be accorded to all nations—including the Central Powers. Special interests should not be recognized by the peace conference if they were incongruent with the general interests of all nations. No special covenants or coalitions would be allowed to function within the framework of the proposed league of nations. Only the league would be permitted to declare international boycotts or economic sanctions. Lastly, all international agreements must be made known to the rest of the world.[47] The Five Particulars immediately joined the Fourteen Points and the Four Principles as integral war aims of the United States.

Couched in the grand Wilsonian manner, the speech attempted to counteract some of the adverse currents of opinion which, from the American point of view, seemed to threaten the integrity of the peace settlement. It stiffened the American attitude toward the Central Powers while continuing to hold out the prospect of a just peace. Directed not only against German militarism but also against Allied imperialism, the speech was another appeal to progressive opinion around the world. It was, in short, a powerful reaction to the Austrian peace feeler.[48]

Responding to a request from President Wilson for frank criticism of the speech, Arthur Balfour commented in detail on the Five Particulars. He thought more than a league was needed to control aggressors. He suggested that the borders of Europe would require revision in order to minimize "the great occasions for wars." Balfour wanted to destroy German dreams of global hegemony. He did not think constitutional reform in Germany and the President's admirable principles would preclude disturbances in the future.[49] Although friendly in tone, the message conveyed distinct distaste for the Wilsonian outlook. The mood of Europe was running counter to the President's desires. The pessimistic appraisals of European intentions made by Colonel House and General Bliss seemed validated by events as the war came to its end during October and November 1918.

Never completely submerged by the war, American distrust of her associates was heightened by events during the summer and fall of 1918. The French agitation for an offensive in Macedonia seemed particularly divorced from American interests. Both the military and the political leadership of the United States began to support affirmative action which would inhibit European subversion of a Wilsonian peace. As American military power and political prestige grew apace in 1918, the President manifested an increasing propensity to dominate the peace settlement. The announcement of the Five Particulars symbolized this development. In military matters the United States continued to support the western strategy and to oppose diversionary operations in subsidiary theaters. American policy and strategy were designed to bring about the defeat of Germany in the shortest possible time while at the same time avoiding diplomatic entanglements which might prejudice the President's plans for the peace.

CHAPTER 8

The Pre-Armistice Negotiations

THE First World War was a limited war. The contending powers never completely dismissed the possibility of a negotiated peace. The impassable gulf which divided the warring coalitions during World War II did not develop during the earlier conflict. When in October 1918 the German leaders realized that victory had slipped from their grasp, they turned to diplomacy in order to salvage as much as possible from defeat. The Allied leaders proved willing to treat for peace if clear-cut guarantees were obtained to insure against a resumption of hostilities.

In relative terms, the United States and Great Britain did not differ fundamentally in their conceptions of the peace settlement, although distinctive areas of disagreement on territorial settlements existed. Together they constituted a restraining influence on the vengeful French and the grasping Italians. Britain, however, had signed a series of "secret treaties" with other Entente Powers which imposed distinct limitations on her diplomacy, and British imperialism in Africa and Asia created Anglo-American tensions. President Wilson's strenuous efforts to maintain diplomatic independence enabled the United States to discuss the peace settlement with both the Central Powers and the Entente Powers unencumbered by imperial commitments of a territorial nature or by binding treaties with other nations.

The American government consistently had envisioned a negotiated peace, once the Central Powers were forced by military action to accept the minimal conditions advanced by the Western coalition. In order to stiffen the morale of the Entente Powers, the President temporarily halted his unilateral pronouncements of war aims after the onset of the German offensive in March 1918, but he did not abandon the idea of a negotiated peace. In September, when the tide had turned in France, the President resumed his personal "peace offensive" with the announcement of the Five Particulars. The impending collapse of Germany, coupled with the growth of American military power, brightened prospects for German acceptance of a Wilsonian design for the future.

The President had to obtain the support of the Allies as well as that of the Central Powers. His policy of maintaining diplomatic independence enabled him to avoid entangling commitments, but it also limited his ability to gain support for his program among the Entente Powers. He believed the course of the war would constantly strengthen American power and his personal prestige. He thought he would be able to dominate events when a cessation of hostilities became feasible.

In September and October the President engaged in an exchange of notes with both Germany and Austria-Hungary, which ultimately committed the principal Central Powers to the Fourteen Points and other Wilsonian pronouncements as a political basis for the peace settlement. When the Central Powers accepted the American terms, Colonel House went to Europe in order to gain Allied acceptance of the President's negotiations and to participate in the development of military and naval terms of the armistice. The Supreme War Council conducted the prearmistice negotiations beginning in Paris late in October.

The discussion of the President's program, along with the determination of the military and naval terms of the Armistice, was the climactic episode in the history of the Supreme War Council.

PRESIDENT WILSON'S NEGOTIATIONS WITH THE CENTRAL POWERS, OCTOBER 1918

After Bulgaria had been defeated on the Macedonian Front, Ludendorff and the other German commanders realized that they would have to ask for an armistice. A change in the German government brought Prince Max of Baden, a political moderate supposedly acceptable to the Western Powers, to the office of Chancellor. On 5 October Prince Max announced to the Reichstag a series of democratizing reforms and the dispatch to the United States of a peace proposal based on the Fourteen Points and other pronouncements of President Wilson—by now protean in character.[1]

In his reply of 8 October, President Wilson did not agree to the proposed armistice, but he held out the prospect of further discussion. The American note posed some highly pertinent questions. Would the peace conference merely discuss the implementation of the Fourteen Points and other additional points, it being assumed that Germany accepted the entire Wilsonian program in principle? Was the Chancellor speaking for his people or only for the leaders who had so far conducted German policy? A necessary condition of the armistice would be the withdrawal of the German army from all occupied areas.[2]

The Austrian note of 16 September and the German note of 5 October stirred great uneasiness in Entente chanceries. Some Allied statesmen wanted to force the President to cease his exchange of notes with the governments of the Central Powers. Others thought he should be conciliated.[3] The prime ministers of Britain, France, and Italy met in Paris on 7 October to discuss the situation. During this meeting, which was not an official session of the Supreme War Council, they drew up a list of eight conditions which they thought should be included in the armistice.[4] These conditions were submitted to a joint meeting of the military representatives and the naval representatives of the Allied Naval Council. The conditions concerned only the military and naval terms of the armistice, not its political basis.

The joint meeting, held on 8 October, developed a number of specific recommendations which reflected the profound distrust of Germany prevailing in professional military and naval circles. General Bliss, ill with influenza, was unable to attend. The naval representatives called for the internment of all German surface vessels along with sixty submarines. The enemy was to report the location of all mine fields and was to evacuate ports on the English Channel, the Mediterranean Sea, and the Black Sea. Helgoland would be surrendered. The military representatives demanded immediate repatriation of prisoners of war and a prohibition on the destruction of materials during the evacuation of occupied territory. Certain fortifications, including Metz and Strasbourg, were to be surrendered, and enemy aircraft were to be concentrated in specified locations during the armistice. The naval blockade of the Central Powers would continue, and Germany would have to fulfill the terms of the armistice within one month after its signature.[5] The joint meeting did not make political recommendations.

General Bliss refused to sign the joint resolution produced by the conferees on the ground that he had no instructions from his government.[6] Bliss personally disliked the joint resolution because in his opinion the peace settlement had to be built on the cornerstone of disarmament. Reporting on the joint resolution to Secretary Baker, he noted: "Judging from the spirit which seems more and more to actuate our European allies, I am beginning to despair that the war will accomplish more than the abolition of *German* militarism while leaving *European* militarism as rampant as ever." A league of nations, spearheaded by the United States and based on disarmament, was, he thought, the only antidote to continued international instability. Bliss had the national interest in mind: "We want to guarantee ourselves against the necessity of having to take up the burden [of armament] under which Europe, and not Germany alone, has been staggering." He reiterated his distrust of the Allies: "What guarantee have we that if we crush one giant out of a dozen some one of the others may not acquire his powers and with his powers his spirit and use his giant strength like a giant?"[7]

The President's political advisors in Washington developed parallel attitudes. Joseph M. Tumulty, Wilson's faithful private secretary, urged the President to counteract what he conceived to be the baneful effects of Entente recalcitrance. Tumulty wanted to take steps which would contribute to "the up-building of liberal opinion in this country . . . the strengthening of your hand at the peace table and . . . the attrition of those forces in the Allied countries which are so grudgingly holding out against your idealistic policies."[8] The belief that European politicians wished to frustrate American plans profoundly influenced American policy throughout the critical negotiations of October and November.

Writing to General March, Bliss perhaps caught the American temper most eloquently:

> I think I told you some time ago that I heard a gentle-

> man in high position here say that the United States was building a bridge for the Allies to pass over; that the time for the United States to secure acquiescence in its wishes was while the bridge was building; that after the Allies had crossed over the bridge they would have no further use for it or its builders. This may be true or not. I do not know.[9]

This mood certainly did not engender smooth relations with the Allies.

During their Paris gathering early in October, the prime ministers sent two messages to Washington. One urged the President to send an American delegate to Europe to participate in the pre-armistice negotiations. The other presented their attitude toward the projected settlement.[10] The latter note was a transparent warning against a unilateral agreement to negotiate an armistice with Germany.[11] This action reflected the European fear that President Wilson might commit the Western coalition without prior consultation. The British government made separate representations of a similar nature on 13 October.[12]

On 12 October Prince Max sent a second message to President Wilson replying to the first American note. Germany, he said, accepted the Fourteen Points and other pronouncements in principle. The peace conference "would be only to agree upon practical details of the application of these terms." He spoke, he concluded, for the German government and for the German people.[13] On the same day Turkey sued for peace on the basis of the Fourteen Points. Each of the Central Powers had now requested an armistice, but only Bulgaria had actually capitulated. Franchet d'Espérey's arrangements with the Bulgarians did not mention the Fourteen Points.[14]

Evidently influenced by European criticism, President

Wilson replied to the German note in sharp tones. The Allies, he said, would determine the nature of evacuation procedures. (Prince Max had attempted to indicate methods of evacuation.) The Allies would conclude an armistice only if it assured against a resumption of hostilities. The note ended with an ominous reminder that the United States had entered the war to destroy arbitrary power, and that peace would depend on assurances that this aim had been attained. This observation was an obvious request for the abdication of Kaiser Wilhelm and the resignation of other reactionary leaders.[15] Unlike the first American note to Germany, this message was well received in Europe. It served the President's purposes well because it crystallized the guarantees expected of Germany but continued to hold out the prospect of a negotiated peace.

Prince Max replied on 20 October, making the concessions demanded by President Wilson. He outlined a sweeping program of reform for Germany, based on changes in the suffrage and enhanced powers for the Reichstag.[16] The British by this time were thoroughly alarmed by the President's progress. Balfour asked Wilson to make no further commitments until inter-Allied consultations resolved certain problems. The British thought the Germans wanted a breathing spell in order to regroup their army for future hostilities.[17] With every new note the Allies became more and more disturbed.

The President was now satisfied with the German position. On 23 October he informed Prince Max that he intended to submit the entire correspondence to the Allies. If the Entente Powers agreed to an armistice, it would be based on the commitments already made by Germany. The note concluded with a threat that the Allies and the United States would demand an unconditional surrender if they had to deal with German militarism rather than a responsible German government.[18] A few days later the Germans accepted this note.[19] Meanwhile Austria-Hungary accepted a revision of one of the Fourteen Points dealing with suppressed nationalities within the Empire and also agreed to negotiate an armistice.[20] Turkey, in a state of complete collapse, was attempting to arrange an armistice through the British admiral commanding the Allied fleet in the eastern Mediterranean.[21]

The stage thus was set for a pre-armistice conference to determine the terms to be offered the Central Powers. The Supreme War Council gathered in Paris for this purpose. Colonel House was sent to represent the United States on the Council, a step which ended the President's policy of avoiding political representation at Versailles. The time had come to secure a Wilsonian peace settlement. Arriving in Paris on 26 October, House faced the most crucial negotiations of his career. Adroit diplomacy would be required to commit the Allies to the Fourteen Points. Unless Colonel House performed at the height of his capacity, the Wilsonian plan for the peace—in many ways an internationalized version of the American dream—would fail to gain acceptance.

THE PRE-ARMISTICE NEGOTIATIONS: MILITARY AND NAVAL TERMS

When Colonel House began his conversations with the leaders of the Allied Powers, he possessed two important supports; the idealism of the Wilsonian program and the power of the American armed forces. American avoidance of diplomatic entanglements was about to bear fruit. The bargaining position of the United States was very strong, and Colonel House permitted himself few errors in judgment. House's principal concern when dealing with the military and naval terms of the armistice was to insure against a possible resumption of hostilities. Often he sought to reconcile controversies which developed between the French and the British. House did not think the arguments over military and naval terms would deadlock the pre-armistice discussions. The fundamental problem for him was to gain inter-Allied indorsement of the President's views. If he succeeded, he believed Wilson could control the peace conference.

General Bliss gave far more thought than House to the military terms of the armistice. He continued to mature his conviction that European militarism was at the heart of the world's troubles and that far-reaching disarmament was the only logical course to pursue.[22] When House arrived in Europe, Bliss sent him a memorandum stressing the need to separate military from political considerations during discussions of the armistice in order to frustrate the desires of the European militarists. He wanted the armistice to require total demobilization and disarmament, along with a German agreement to submit to all arrangements deemed proper by the victors.[23] House chose to ignore Bliss' interesting but politically unfeasible proposals.

A conference of generals held by Foch at Senlis on 25 October revealed a divergence of military opinion concerning the terms of the armistice. Foch pointed out to his colleagues—Pétain, Haig, and Pershing— that the armistice must render Germany powerless to resume hostilities. Pershing called for unconditional surrender, thus taking the most extreme position possible. Haig then advocated a relatively moderate set of terms which he thought would insure German capitulation. He feared that excessive demands would stiffen German resistance. Foch expressed a preference for more stringent terms, arguing that the Germans had been badly defeated and that "nothing gives wings to an army like victory." Pétain presented a detailed list of terms which reflected the uncompromising attitude of the French. Pershing followed with an even stricter set, apparently offering them as an alternative to unconditional surrender. The conferees must have assumed that he had given up his earlier proposal. Despite French and American pressure, Haig refused to withdraw his suggestions.[24]

After this meeting Foch presented his recommendations to Clemenceau. They closely paralleled those given by Pétain at Senlis.[25] Thus the basis for the pre-armistice discussion of military terms had been created. The recommendations of Foch plus the joint resolution adopted by the military representatives and the naval representatives served to guide the negotiations of the statesmen on the Supreme War Council.

General Pershing refused to accept the terms of Foch without a public display of irritation. In a message to the War Department he called for a severer armistice than that recommended by the Allied commander-in-chief.[26] Secretary Baker immediately cabled the President's reaction to Pershing's message. In general, the President preferred a moderate armistice. He wanted guarantees against a resumption of the fighting, but he did not wish to humiliate Germany unduly, an action that might strengthen the hand of the militarists in Berlin.[27] This message certainly constituted a rebuke to Pershing. It was a clear hint to the General to change his opinions. The President wanted to place necessary restraints on Germany, but he did not wish to give the European Allies undue advantages over the Central Powers.

In a message to Colonel House the President put his policy more candidly. "My deliberate judgment," he wrote, "is that our whole weight should be thrown for an armistice which will prevent a renewal of hostilities by Germany but which will be as moderate as possible within those limits, because it is certain that too much success or security on the part of the Allies will make a genuine peace settlement exceedingly difficult if not impossible."[28] This sentence reiterated the President's oft-expressed suspicions of European motives.

General Pershing created an irritating contretemps by submitting an unauthorized letter to the Supreme War Council advocating unconditional surrender.[29] This curious example of military meddling in a clearly political situation did not lead to serious consequences. Secretary Baker was particularly outraged by Pershing's act, although normally he gave the General his wholehearted support. Baker notified the President that Pershing had placed himself "on record one way with you and another way with the Supreme War Council. It is really tragic."[30] Colonel House retrieved the potentially embarrassing situation by informing Pershing that decisions concerning the armistice terms were political in nature. Pershing did not retract his views, but they did not figure in the succeeding negotiations.[31] House recommended that the President drop the matter since the letter had been removed from consideration. Secretary Baker composed a severe reprimand which he proposed to send to Pershing, but the President gently vetoed this step after considering House's recommendation.[32]

Meanwhile the naval leaders had also discussed armistice terms. Germany had ordered an end to unrestricted submarine warfare, but many other naval matters concerned the Allies.[33] The British desire for stringent naval terms met with strong German resistance. Thus the roles taken in connection with military terms were reversed during the discussion of naval terms. The British wanted to eliminate the German threat to their naval supremacy, whereas France wanted to destroy Germany's capacity to wage a war on the land against other continental powers.

The punitive British terms called for the surrender or demobilization of almost the entire German fleet, along with the continuance of the blockade.[34] Foch balked at this program, fearing that Germany would refuse to accept it. His attitude paralleled the reaction of Haig to the military terms desired by France. Foch wanted merely to intern the German surface fleet in neutral ports.

Finally, Lloyd George and Admiral William S. Benson, the American Chief of Naval Operations, proposed a compromise whereby a great portion of the German surface fleet would be interned in neutral ports, while most of the submarine fleet would be surrendered outright to the Allies. Colonel House lent his support to this arrangement.[35] The terms suggested earlier by Admiral William S. Sims, the American naval commander in European waters, reflected the relatively passive attitude of the United States. Sims had called for internment of the German fleet, restrictions on mining, evacuation of occupied ports, and continuance of the blockade.[36] Because the American position on naval terms was moderate, Colonel House and Admiral Benson were able to serve as compromisers between the French and the British.

Colonel House reflected no desire to dominate the discussion of military and naval terms. He functioned primarily as a mediator. Seeking to fulfill the President's desire for a moderate settlement, he adopted a flexible position midway between the French and the British, continually seeking to compose differences of opinion. House approved the final terms because, by and large, the President's desires had been met.

The rising fear that severe armistice terms might precipitate Bolshevik revolutions in Germany and Austria-Hungary appears to have influenced the final decisions of the Supreme War Council. The American chargé in Sweden had reported this possibility to the State Department, but Lansing dismissed it as clever propaganda by Germany designed to lessen the severity of the terms.[37] House discussed this matter with Lloyd George and Clemenceau, indicating his belief that onerous requirements might cause domestic upheaval in Germany. He probably advanced this argument to strengthen his case for relatively merciful terms. In any case, he adverted to the Bolshevik menace several times during the discussions in Paris. House even asked his fellow negotiators if they feared revolutions in their own countries. Clemenceau vigorously rejected the likelihood of revolt in France, but Lloyd George conceded the possibility of unrest in Britain. Both agreed that revolution could easily occur in Italy.[38] The State Department continued to receive intimations of Bolshevik gains in Germany, but this information does not appear to have vitally influenced American policy.[39]

The important negotiations in Paris were undertaken outside the regular meetings of the Supreme War Council. The official meetings, which began on 31 October, merely created a formal record of what had been decided privately. This pragmatic approach allowed a freedom of expression which otherwise would have been impossible.

On 1 November the Supreme War Council officially accepted a list of military terms substantially in accord with those recommended by Marshal Foch. Prime Minister Lloyd George yielded to the French rather than jeopardize the chance for an armistice before winter. Obviously he expected a French *quid pro quo* when the naval terms came before the Council. The military terms met the desires of the President, but neither Bliss nor Pershing, for entirely different reasons, was pleased with them.[40]

The Council did not approve the naval terms until its last meeting on 4 November. Further discussions of naval terms centered on whether the German surface fleet should be interned or surrendered outright. The formula worked out by Lloyd George and Admiral Benson represented a compromise which assuaged the French while insuring that Germany would suffer eclipse as a leading naval power. The naval terms provided for the surrender of the submarine fleet, the continuance of the naval blockade, and the disarmament and internment of ten battleships, six heavy cruisers, eight light cruisers, and fifty destroyers. The provision for internment actually placed the task of disposing of the German fleet in the hands of the peace conference. This fact pleased Admiral Benson, always suspicious of the British, since it guaranteed that the United States could block efforts to transfer the German vessels to the navies of the Entente.[41]

After the Supreme War Council had adjourned, Colonel House recorded in his diary a remark he had made to Sir Eric Geddes, the British First Lord of the Admiralty. House "frankly told him that I preferred the resolution offered by George which we adopted, but that I would [in any case] have followed England in the naval terms as I had followed Marshal Foch in the military terms."[42] House's tactic of supporting the French and the British in their principal desires had resulted in a lessening of the severity of both the military and naval terms. Thus realistically the flexible House managed to fulfill the President's wish for terms which would prepare the ground for a just peace.

The Supreme War Council had accommodated a most delicate series of negotiations and had produced terms acceptable to the several protagonists in Paris. A year's experience with inter-Allied issues of a political-military nature had trained the Council well for the preparation of armistice terms. In its final moments the institution had come of age.

THE PRE-ARMISTICE NEGOTIATIONS: THE POLITICAL SETTLEMENT

The Supreme War Council discussed the political basis of the armistice concurrently with the military and naval terms. Contrary to his behavior during other phases of the discussions, Colonel House pursued an intensely active course during the political conferences. He had come to Paris primarily to gain inter-Allied acceptance of President Wilson's Fourteen Points, and he proved capable of exerting sustained pressure in order to accomplish his ends.

When the Fourteen Points were announced in January 1918, they were thought of in Europe primarily as part of the American propaganda effort against the Central Powers. There had been rumblings of discontent, but the general reaction had not been particularly violent. As time passed and the President's intentions became clearer, European criticism of the Fourteen Points began to mount.[43] The phraseology of the Points rendered them susceptible to diverse interpretations. The inter-Allied discussion of them centered on interpretations rather than on the general principles contained in them. The individual countries became preoccupied with points that affected them adversely rather than with the entire list. The controversies which ensued during the pre-armistice negotiations stemmed from the President's unwillingness to alter the Fourteen Points in detail or to accept views not in accord with his own wishes. His reluctance to express concrete personal interpretations added to the general confusion which prevailed in Europe.[44] Before Colonel House arrived in Paris, various indications of Allied opposition to some of the points filtered to the State Department.[45]

Colonel House soon discovered that the Entente leaders hoped to by-pass the Fourteen Points despite the President's prior negotiations with the Central Powers. On 29

October, the prime ministers, the foreign ministers, and Colonel House—sitting as an unofficial steering committee of the Supreme War Council—took up the Fourteen Points for the first time. Clemenceau immediately objected to the provision for open covenants openly arrived at, and Lloyd George followed with arguments against the principle of freedom of the seas. Then Sonnino abruptly proposed that the armistice deal only with military and naval terms.[46] The Italian Foreign Minister's suggestion was a blatant effort to circumvent the American desire to offer an armistice to Germany with the understanding that postwar negotiations would be based on President Wilson's program. House now was convinced that the Allied leaders wanted to take control of the peace negotiations and frustrate President Wilson's plans.[47] House believed that American bargaining power would decline after the end of hostilities, and he deemed it necessary to gain inter-Allied acceptance of the Fourteen Points during the pre-armistice negotiations.

The Colonel immediately reminded the prime ministers that rejection of the Fourteen Points would mean repudiation of the President's negotiations with the Central Powers. Clemenceau then said that such a development might lead to a separate peace between the United States and the Central Powers. To this probe House replied significantly: "It might." This remark, he reported later, had an "exciting effect" on the gathering. After further comments on the Fourteen Points, the conferees decided to draw up separate commentaries on them in order to prepare for future negotiations.[48]

On the same day Lloyd George suggested to House that the United States accept a mandate over German East Africa. Other German possessions in Africa and Asia would be transferred to South Africa and Australia. France and

Britain would discharge certain obligations in the Middle East. House interpreted the Prime Minister's suggestion as an attempt to enlist support for British efforts to placate the Dominions and establish France and Britain as dominant powers in the Middle East.[49] This episode strengthened House's feeling that the Entente hoped to circumvent the President's peace plans.

Having anticipated a claim that the Fourteen Points were too vague to serve as a political basis for the armistice, Colonel House had asked Frank Cobb and Walter Lippmann to prepare an explanation of them. Cobb and Lippmann were both journalists who enjoyed the confidence of House. The President authorized the Colonel to use this commentary or "gloss" during his negotiations provided its contents were considered illustrative rather than binding. The gloss played an important part during the rest of the session of the Supreme War Council, House insisting that it destroyed the argument that the Fourteen Points were too vague.[50]

President Wilson manifested increasing irritation as Entente opposition developed in Paris. On 29 October he sent House an indignant message trenchantly announcing his policy:

> Can be no real difficulty about peace terms and interpretation of fourteen points if the Entente Statesmen will be perfectly frank with us and have no selfish aims of their own which would in any case alienate us from them altogether. It is the fourteen points that Germany has accepted. England cannot dispense with our friendship in the future and the other Allies cannot without our assistance get their rights as against England. If it is the purpose of the statesmen to nullify my influence force the purpose boldly to the surface and let me speak of it boldly to all the world as I shall. League of nations underlies freedom of the seas and every other part of peace program so far as

> I am concerned. I am ready to repudiate any selfish programme openly, but assume that the Allies cannot honorably turn the present discussions into a peace conference without me.[51]

The Colonel could hardly have obtained a more powerful document. The message indicates the strength of the American bargaining position and the depth of the President's emotional commitment to his plans.

Colonel House decided the time had come to play his strongest card, a threat to take the United States out of the war unless the Entente Powers accepted the Fourteen Points. He told the President of his scheme on 30 October:

> It is my intention to tell the Prime Ministers today that if their conditions of peace are essentially different from the conditions you have laid down and for which the American people have been fighting, that you will probably feel obliged to go before Congress and state the new conditions and ask for their advice as to whether the United States shall continue to fight for the aims of Great Britain, France, and Italy.
>
> The last thing they want is publicity and they do not wish it to appear that there is any difference between the Allies. Unless we deal with these people with a firm hand everything we have been fighting for will be lost. . . .
>
> I feel confident that we must play a very strong hand and if it meets with your approval I will do it in the gentlest and friendliest way possible.[52]

The Colonel knew that the Allies could not stand the shock of an unceremonious American withdrawal from the war. In addition to his proposed threat, House also suggested that the United States begin to exert economic pressure by reducing shipments to Europe of manpower, food, money, and materials.

Later that day House met privately with Clemenceau,

Lloyd George, and Orlando in order to resume discussion of the Fourteen Points. The Colonel quietly dropped his bombshell. Later he described the incident in his report to the President. Repeating the details of the statement he had previously communicated to President Wilson, House noted: "As soon as I said this Lloyd George and Clemenceau looked at each other significantly."[53] Each of the prime ministers had prepared commentaries on the Fourteen Points, but after House's announcement Clemenceau withdrew his statement and accepted the document prepared by Lloyd George. House had won his point.

The British took exception to only two of the Points. Lloyd George sought to preserve complete freedom of action on the question of freedom of the seas (Point II). He specifically asked for "compensation," a euphemism for reparations, to repay the Allies for injuries to civilians and their property (Point VIII). Sonnino wanted to argue the question of Italian borders (Point IX), but Orlando overruled him.[54] House embraced the compromise proposed by Lloyd George and accordingly urged the President to accept it.[55] On 31 October he explained his reasons:

> Everything is changing for the better since yesterday.... If you will give me a free hand in dealing with these immediate negotiations, I can assure you that nothing will be done to embarrass you or to compromise any of your peace principles. You will have as free a hand after the armistice as you now have. It is exceedingly important that nothing be said or done at this time which may in any way halt the armistice which will save so many thousands of lives. Negotiations are now proceeding satisfactorily.[56]

Although the British reservations highly irritated the President, he ultimately accepted the Colonel's advice. House was ordered to obtain acceptance of freedom of the seas at least in principle.[57] House, however, could obtain only an agreement to discuss the issue at the peace conference.[58] In a message to Colonel House the President threatened to "build up the strongest navy our resources permit" if the British proved unwilling to rely on American friendship and good faith, but nothing could budge Lloyd George further.[59]

The reservation concerning reparations also stirred further controversy. Clemenceau finally succeeded in incorporating a phrase into the armistice agreement which modified Point VIII: "Any future claims or demands on the part of the Allies remain unaffected."[60] This proviso opened the door to the tremendous reparations imposed upon Germany by the Treaty of Versailles. Colonel House decided not to protest strongly. He had gained most of what he had sought, and he wanted to avoid holding up the conclusion of the armistice by making further demands.

On 4 November the final meeting of the Supreme War Council approved the text of the so-called "Pre-Armistice Agreement." This document was a letter sent to President Wilson which specified the political basis of the armistice to be offered to Germany. It committed the United States to negotiate a treaty based on the Fourteen Points, the Four Principles, and the Five Particulars, subject only to the reservations concerning freedom of the seas and reparations.[61] Colonel House had achieved a notable diplomatic triumph. He could not resist sending a cable to President Wilson pointing out the significance of the Pre-Armistice Agreement:

> I consider that we have won a great diplomatic victory. . . . This has been done in the face of a hostile and influential junta in the United States and the thoroughly unsympathetic personnel constituting the Entente Governments.
>
> I doubt whether any of the heads of the governments

with whom we have been dealing quite recognize how far they are now committed to the American peace program.[62]

The Colonel's circumspect but powerful diplomacy had given the President the strongest possible bargaining position from which to meet his fellow peacemakers. If the Fourteen Points and the supplementary pronouncements had not been accepted by the Entente prior to the armistice with Germany, the President would have come to Paris for the peace conference without a legal basis for the program he had so carefully and persistently expounded to the world during the period of American belligerency.

The pre-armistice negotiations were the last important actions of the Supreme War Council. Its consultative apparatus had succeeded in coping with the most delicate subject to come before it during its short existence. Any analysis of the pre-armistice negotiations should take into consideration the institutional characteristics of the Council and its evolution prior to November 1918.

The dispatch of Colonel House to Paris in October 1918 symbolized a great reorientation in American political-military strategy. President Wilson previously eschewed political participation in the inter-Allied consultations conducted at Versailles, but events had imposed the necessity of committing the Entente Powers to the American peace program prior to the end of hostilities with the Central Powers. While in Paris Colonel House achieved both of his ends—a set of military and naval terms which met the President's desire for some degree of moderation, and a pre-armistice agreement which committed the Allies to a Wilsonian peace.

On 10 November Colonel House dispatched a message

to President Wilson which revealed both his satisfaction with the negotiations in Paris and his prevision of the difficult months to come:

> I would suggest when the armistice is signed that you read its terms to Congress and use the occasion to give another message to the world. You have a right to assume that the two great features of the armistice are the defeat of German military imperialism and the acceptance by the allied Powers of the kind of peace the world has longed for. A steadying note seems to me necessary at this time. A word of warning and a word of hope should be said. The World is in a ferment and Civilization itself is wavering in the balance.[63]

Rarely had a great nation followed a course so consistently and seemingly achieved its ends so fully. During 1918 the United States had gained its military goal—the defeat of Germany—and its immediate political goal—the provisional acceptance of President Wilson's plans for the postwar world. The United States benefited from the activities of the Supreme War Council and suffered few setbacks. If disillusionment hovered in the future, the Western coalition had gained a series of remarkable successes in 1918.

CONCLUSION

Throughout the period of American belligerency during World War I, American relations with the Entente turned on two fundamental objectives, a clear-cut victory over the Central Powers and the maintenance of American diplomatic independence. President Wilson deemed both objectives necessary in order to insure the fulfillment of his plans for the postwar world. The American distrust of Europe and Europe's ways—born of the colonial experience, matured during the revolutionary generation, and deepened by the long period of comparative noninvolvement in international affairs during the nineteenth century—inevitably strengthened American fears respecting the intentions of the Allies as well as those of the Central Powers. Extraordinarily reluctant to commit the United States to war, Wilson atoned for his deed by converting the final phase of World War I into a war to make the world safe for democracy. This crusade culminated in the plan for a league of nations. In Clemenceau, Orlando, Lloyd George, and other Allied leaders the President discerned a cynicism as undesirable as that reflected in German policy.

During 1917, President Wilson gave precedence to military preparations for the support of the Allies. At this important stage, he avoided diplomatic involvements as well as unilateral pronouncements which might materially lessen his influence on the peace settlement as well as injure the military effort. He believed American prestige would expand over time as the Allies came to rely more and more extensively on American aid in order to defeat the German coalition. In 1918, as American bargaining power increased, he continued to avoid diplomatic commitments to the Allies but issued a series of comprehensive unilateral statements which clearly if generally exposed his war aims and peace plans to the world. As the war ended, he was able to commit both the Allies and the Central Powers to his proposals for the peace settlement, the former because they had become largely dependent upon the United States and the latter because they discerned in the President's program the most magnanimous settlement possible in defeat.

The history of American participation in the affairs of the Supreme War Council clearly reflects Wilsonian purposes. Lloyd George, the real progenitor of the Council, hoped that it would unify over-all Allied strategy and policy for 1918 in order to withstand the final offensive efforts of the German army in France. The United States, definitely interested in an efficient military effort, supported coordination of inter-Allied military effort through the Council but feared the political consequences of the Lloyd George plan. Consequently, General Bliss became a military representative at the Supreme War Council but no political delegate was appointed. At Versailles, General Bliss did all he could to assist in arranging a coordinated inter-Allied strategy against the Central Powers, but he operated within the bounds of two fundamental premises; he adhered closely to the strategy of concentrating the American army in France, and he avoided actions which might have entailed undesirable political consequences for the President. The United States supported the unified command because it was thought necessary to coordinate inter-Allied military power. On the other hand, the United States resisted all efforts to amalgamate American soldiers into European formations, not only because the proposal implied American military inferiority but also because it might have weakened American bargaining power at the peace conference after victory. In the case of intervention in Russia, the United States remained intransigently opposed until July 1918 (and then vastly restricted the scope of the inter-Allied effort) not only because the plans for intervention violated the strategy of concentration against Germany in France but also because the projects seemed fraught with manifold political dangers. In most instances during 1918, the United States cooperated heartily with the Allies and the Supreme War Council in military and diplomatic endeavors which did not appear to prejudice the President's projects for the postwar world, but when inter-Allied proposals seemed to involve unwanted political consequences or military commitments which seemed impractical or unnecessary, General Bliss refused to lend American aid and comfort.

The Wilsonian wartime effort culminated with almost complete success in November 1918. During October, the Central Powers agreed to an armistice on the basis of the Fourteen Points and associated pronouncements. Colonel House then achieved inter-Allied acceptance of the Wilsonian program at the pre-armistice conference of the Supreme War Council in Paris. Events had proceeded according to plan. The Central Powers had been decisively defeated, and the Entente had been forced to accept American leadership in making the peace. The United States had made an indispensable military contribution and had retained diplomatic independence. President Wilson had reached the height of his prestige, and the future seemed bright indeed. Who then could have predicted the tragedy of Versailles and after?

Notes, Annotated Bibliography, and Index

Notes

The two principal collections of documents relating to the Supreme War Council are both in the National Archives. One group, by far the more comprehensive, is in the War Department Archives. The other group is in the State Department Archives. In the following notes these collections are designated as follows:

SWC-WDA means "Records of the Supreme War Council, War Department Archives."

SWC-SDA means "Records of the Supreme War Council, State Department Archives."

CHAPTER 1: *American Intervention in World War I*

1. "The Scheme of Organization of a Supreme War Council," 7 November 1917, reprinted in Charles Seymour, ed., *The Intimate Papers of Colonel House,* III, *Into the World War* (Boston, 1928), 246.

2. There is no full-scale study of the Supreme War Council. Neither is there a general account of inter-Allied cooperation during World War I. The closest approach is the study of Sir Frederick B. Maurice, *Lessons of Allied Co-operation: Naval, Military, and Air, 1914-1918* (New York, 1942)—a useful but incomplete treatment. A pioneer study of the Supreme War Council is an unpublished doctoral dissertation completed at the University of Virginia by Thomas Daniel Shumate, Jr., "The Allied Supreme War Council 1917-1918," (1952).

The best contemporary account of American participation in the Supreme War Council is the "Final Report" of General Tasker H. Bliss, military representative of the United States, presented to the

Secretary of State on 19 February 1920. It is reprinted in *Papers Relating to the Foreign Relations of the United States: The Lansing Papers* (Washington, 1940), II, 199-303.

3. This comment was recorded later by Colonel House. Diary of Colonel Edward M. House, 4 January 1917, Edward M. House Papers, Yale University Library, New Haven, Connecticut.

4. Woodrow Wilson, *The Public Papers of Woodrow Wilson: War and Peace* (New York, 1927), I, 8, 16.

5. An interesting study of the unconscious motivations which appear to have animated the war leaders is A. L. George and J. L. George, *Woodrow Wilson and Colonel House: A Personality Study* (New York, 1956).

6. Wilson, *Public Papers: War and Peace,* I, 9-11.

7. On 31 March 1917 General Tasker H. Bliss, the Assistant Chief of Staff, forwarded a memorandum from the Army War College to General Hugh Scott, the Chief of Staff, urging that some agreement be made with the Entente prior to the declaration of war, specifying common ends. This recommendation was not acted upon. Bliss to Scott, 31 March 1917, Tasker H. Bliss Papers, Library of Congress, Washington, D.C.

8. Professor Seymour, the editor of the House Papers, believes the first use of this term occurred in a letter from the President to Colonel House dated 15 June 1917. *Intimate Papers,* III, 29-30. No official engagements resulted from the visits of the Balfour and Viviani missions. See *ibid.,* 42-50; Balfour to Wilson, 18 May 1918, Woodrow Wilson Papers, Library of Congress, Washington, D.C.; Ray Stannard Baker, *Woodrow Wilson, Life and Letters,* VII, *War Leader* (Garden City, New York, 1939), 42-44.

9. Wilson to House, 21 July 1917, House Papers. Underlining is in original document.

10. Joseph M. Tumulty, Wilson's private secretary, had recommended that the President maintain his diplomatic freedom of action even before the outbreak of hostilities. Tumulty to Wilson, 24 March 1917, Wilson Papers. A secondary motive of some importance was the American desire to avoid irritating relations between France and Britain. Colonel House was sensitive to this problem. In his diary he noted: "Distrust lies close beneath the surface, and a little difference between [France and Britain] would bring it from under cover." Diary, 30 April 1917, House Papers. Foreign Secretary Arthur Balfour maintained his part of the agreement to avoid a public discussion of war aims. See his comment in July when he said that "the immediate duty before us is not to discuss in detail what terms we

9. This exchange is recorded in the minutes of the twelfth meeting of the military representatives, 19 February 1918, SWC-WDA.

10. War College Report, 8 October 1917, forwarded to the Chief of Staff (Bliss), 12 November 1917, SWC-WDA.

11. The President's willingness to support the reform of the Rapallo Agreement is indicated in Wilson to House, 1 December 1917, House Papers.

12. Bliss to Baker, 23 December 1917, Bliss Papers.

13. See the minutes of the third session of the Supreme War Council, 30 January–2 February 1918, SWC-WDA. Some relevant excerpts from the debates are in *U. S. Army in World War*, II, 185-187. See the "Final Report" of General Bliss for information concerning his part in the establishment of the General Reserve. Cf. Palmer, *Bliss, Peacemaker*, 237-240; Foch, *Memoirs*, 240; Pershing, *My Experiences*, I, 310-315.

14. Resolution passed at the fifth meeting of the third session of the Supreme War Council, 2 February 1918, in minutes of the third session, SWC-WDA.

15. "Final Report" of General Bliss, SWC-WDA.

16. *U. S. Army in World War*, II, 192. For a British document specifying British objections to a French generalissimo, see memorandum by Lieutenant Colonel L. S. Amery of the British Section, Supreme War Council, to Sir Edward Carson (undated), SWC-WDA. General Bliss accepted the British point of view in his "Final Report."

17. General Bliss lists the eight meetings of the Executive War Board and summarizes its activities in his "Final Report." The proceedings of the Board are in the Bliss Papers. The composition and disposition of the proposed General Reserve is discussed in Tasker H. Bliss, "The Evolution of the Unified Command," *Foreign Affairs* (December, 1922), I, 19-20.

18. For debates on this subject in the House of Commons, see *Hansard's Parliamentary Debates*, 103 H. C. Deb. 5s., 18-707. A partisan comment favorable to Lloyd George is Peter Wright, *At the Supreme War Council* (New York, 1921). A critique of the Prime Minister is in Maurice, *Lessons of Allied Co-operation*, 123. Lloyd George's own account is in his *War Memoirs*, V, 285-324. The constitutional issues raised by Robertson are discussed in Bliss, *Foreign Affairs*, I, 16-17. Robertson mentioned the constitutional difficulty to Bliss when the latter was in Europe with the House Mission in 1917. Report of General Bliss to the Secretary of War on the House Mission, 18 December 1917, Bliss Papers. Haig's diary on the

period is in Blake, ed., *Private Papers of Douglas Haig*, 283-288.

19. Cable of the Acting Chief of Staff (Biddle), printed in *U. S. Army in World War*, II, 207-208.

20. Bliss to Baker, 21 February 1918, Wilson Papers.

21. *U. S. Army in World War*, II, 228; Maurice, *Lessons of Allied Co-operation*, 122-127; Bliss, *Foreign Affairs*, I, 19-20; minutes of the eighteenth meeting of the military representatives, 28 February 1918, SWC-WDA.

22. Lloyd George believes the anticlerical attitude of Clemenceau was the crucial factor and also suggests that the French Premier had military ambitions. See his *War Memoirs*, V, 356-359. Jere C. King relies on anticlericalism to explain this episode in his *Generals and Politicians*, 205-211. Shumate agrees generally with King, although he raises the issue of Clemenceau's ingrained distrust of the military and emphasizes the activities of Pétain. Shumate, "The Allied Supreme War Council," 526-532. A strong defender of the General Reserve suggests that Pétain and Haig deliberately deceived Foch. L. S. Amery, *My Political Life*, II, *War and Peace, 1914-1929* (London, 1953), 145. For Haig's view at the time, see Blake, ed., *Private Papers of Douglas Haig*, 289-290.

23. Quoted in Bliss to Baker and March, 5 March 1918, SWC-WDA.

24. "Final Report" of General Bliss. The text of the final resolution is quoted in Foch, *Memoirs*, 242.

25. Bliss to Baker and March, 5 March 1918, SWC-WDA. The cable is printed in *Foreign Relations*, 1918, Supplement 1, I, 152.

26. Polk to Page, 11 March 1918, SWC-WDA.

27. Bliss to Rawlinson, 9 March 1918, SWC-WDA.

28. Bliss to March, 10 April 1918, and Bliss to Executive War Board, 9 March 1918, SWC-WDA.

29. Lloyd George, *War Memoirs*, V, 359-360.

30. Resolution on the continuance of the General Reserve, in minutes of the fourth session of the Supreme War Council, 14-15 March 1918, SWC-WDA. General Foch objected strenuously but was overruled. Foch, *Memoirs*, 242-243.

31. The resolution providing for dissolution is in the minutes of the fifth session of the Supreme War Council, 1-2 May 1918,SWC-WDA.

32. The letter of Baker to Bliss, 24 October 1922, is quoted in Palmer, *Baker*, II, 141.

33. Foch, *Memoirs*, 257-258; Bliss to March, 10 April 1918, SWC-WDA.

34. Maurice, *Lessons of Allied Co-operation*, 130-131; Foch, *Memoirs*, 259.

35. Lloyd George, *War Memoirs*, V, 390; Foch, *Memoirs*, 261-264; Pershing, *My Experiences*, I, 312-316. The text of the Doullens Agreement is in *U. S. Army in World War*, II, 254.

36. King thinks the British seriously considered making Clemenceau the commander-in-chief, but he does not believe the French Premier sought the position. King, *Generals and Politicians*, 214-218.

37. Foch, *Memoirs*, 275. The passage is translated and quoted by Lloyd George, *War Memoirs*, VI, *1918*, 4. The Pershing offer is described in Pershing, *My Experiences*, I, 312-316. The President's cable of 29 March 1918 is quoted in Palmer, *Baker*, II, 149. The Secretary of War suggested this gesture in a cable reprinted in *U. S. Army in World War*, II, 264. Lloyd George requested American adherence to the Doullens Agreement. Baker, *Life and Letters*, VIII, 59.

38. On 30 March Foch issued orders providing for the stabilization of the front and the organization of a maneuver force to repulse further attacks or to counterattack. These instructions are reprinted in *U. S. Army in World War*, II, 266-267. They are reminiscent of Foch's plans for the General Reserve.

39. Lloyd George, *War Memoirs*, VI, 11.

40. Copy of Beauvais Agreement, 3 April 1918, SWC-WDA. See also Lloyd George, *War Memoirs*, VI, 11.

41. Bliss to March, 3 April 1918, SWC-WDA; Frazier to Auchincloss, 16 May 1918, House Papers.

42. Minutes of the fifth session of the Supreme War Council, 1-2 May 1918, SWC-WDA; Foch, *Memoirs*, 277-278; Lloyd George *War Memoirs*, VI, 50.

43. Frazier to House, 18 April 1918, House Papers.

44. Wiseman to House, 11 May 1918, House Papers.

45. House to Wilson, 3 June 1918, and House to Bliss, 30 July 1918, House Papers.

46. Bliss to House, 12 September 1918, House Papers.

47. Undated report by Amery on the future of the Supreme War Council, SWC-WDA.

48. Bliss to Baker, 26 June 1918, Bliss Papers.

CHAPTER 5: *Utilization of American Manpower*

1. Baker, *Life and Letters,* VII, 317.

2. Pershing, *My Experiences,* I, 255-256.

3. See the report of General Bliss to Colonel House, 14 December 1917, quoted in part in *Intimate Papers,* III, 303-305. Bliss emphasized the need for a massive reinforcement in 1918. See his Report to the Secretary of War on the House Mission, 18 December 1917, Bliss Papers.

4. See the Colonel's report on the Mission, 14 December 1917, quoted in part in *Intimate Papers,* III, 300-302. The complete report is printed in *Foreign Relations, 1917*, Supplement 2, I, 334-357.

5. Pershing, *My Experiences,* I, 249-250, 254-255; *U. S. Army in World War,* II, 191. Bliss also recommended that twenty-four American divisions should be in Europe by June 1918. Bliss to the Acting Chief of Staff (Biddle), undated but ca. 1 December 1917, Bliss Papers.

6. Note the pressure applied to House by Sir William Wiseman in Wiseman to House, 15 December 1917, House Papers.

7. Baker to Pershing, 18 December 1918, House Papers; *Foreign Relations, 1917,* Supplement 2, I, 356-357.

8. For the General's conversations with the French, see *U. S. Army in World War,* II, 105-107, 117-118. See also *ibid.,* III, 8-9.

9. Poincaré to Wilson, 28 December 1917, Wilson Papers.

10. Pershing to Bliss, 9 January 1918, Baker Papers. A cable of 1 January 1918 expressing approximately the same sentiments is printed in *U. S. Army in World War,* II, 132. Baker supported the American Commander-in-Chief's position in a letter to the President. He reiterated Pershing's opinion that if amalgamation occurred no troops lent to the Allies would return to American command. Baker to Wilson, 3 January 1918, Wilson Papers.

11. See the recommendations of General Fox Conner, head of Pershing's Operations Section (G-3), regarding amalgamation with the British, 16 December 1917. *U. S. Army in World War,* III, 7.

12. Pershing to Baker, 17 January 1918, Pershing Papers. Pershing wrote in part: "Although in serving with the British we should not have differences in language to contend with, the sticking point of the thing is service under another flag. If human beings were pawns it would be different, but they are our own men and we should therefore study very carefully our own national sentiment and the

attitude of our army and the people toward the proposition. Generally speaking the army would be opposed to it."

13. See General Conner's memorandum of 16 April 1918, in *U. S. Army in World War,* II, 283-285. It must be understood that Pershing at this time was seeking out all possible arguments in support of his policy and was attempting to verbalize them. This may explain why Conner recorded what others probably were thinking.

14. Pershing, *My Experiences,* I, 288-289. See also *ibid.*, II, 39.

15. Wilson to Poincaré, 8 January 1918, Wilson Papers.

16. Robertson to Haig, 3 January 1918, in *U. S. Army in World War,* II, 133-134.

17. Pershing to War Department, 13 January 1918, Wilson Papers. See also Palmer, *Baker,* II, 112. It should be noted that Pershing had reached an agreement with Pétain involving the training of certain American units with the French. See the summary of the Pershing-Pétain conversation, 11 January 1918, in *U. S. Army in World War,* II, 155-157.

18. Baker to Wilson, 19 January 1918, Baker Papers.

19. Wilson to Baker, 20 January 1918, R. S. Baker Papers.

20. In his letter Baker indicated that the United States accepted the 150-battalion plan, provided "that the battalions should be recalled for service with our own divisions should it be determined wise to do so; second, that the transportation of these troops shall not interfere with the assistance in tonnage to be provided by the British to carry out our own military programs. . . . In order to avoid any disappointment . . . the utmost care should be taken to have an explicit understanding that these battalions and their transportation are contingent upon the supply of tonnage to us for our agreed minimum military effort." Baker to Bliss, 21 January 1918, SWC-WDA.

General Bliss soon made known his support of the 150-battalion plan and indicated to General Sir Henry Wilson that he would press the matter with his government if the latter thought it necessary. Callwell, *Sir Henry Wilson,* II, 53. Obviously, the Wilson-Baker correspondence indicates that both considered the 150-battalion plan an addition to the American reinforcement over and above the original plan.

21. See Pershing's cable to Bliss, 13 January 1918, in *U. S. Army in World War,* III, 17-18. See another to Bliss, 15 January 1918, quoting a message sent to Robertson stating his favorable attitude if his reservations were accepted. *Ibid.*, 18-19. Pershing had insisted that the British guarantee maximum manpower of their

own in his letter to Robertson. The British War Cabinet accepted the Pershing reservations but pointed out that much British manpower was absorbed by naval and industrial requirements. *Ibid.*, 20. Lloyd George also protested against the other countries' unawareness of drains on British manpower from other than military sources. *War Memoirs,* V, 137-139.

22. Pershing, *My Experiences,* I, 304-305.

23. Palmer, *Bliss, Peacemaker,* 221-222. See the minutes of an Anglo-American military conference held 29 January 1918, during which Bliss stoutly defended General Pershing. *U. S. Army in World War,* III, 29-34.

24. See *ibid.* for details of the meeting with Lloyd George. The details of the early negotiations concerning the six-division program are recounted in a cable from Bliss to Baker, 30 January 1918, in *ibid.*, 35-36. See also the correspondence between Robertson and Pershing concerning the six-division program in *ibid.*, 37-39.

25. See the partial transcript of the American minutes of the Supreme War Council meeting, 30 January 1918, in *ibid.*, II, 185-187.

26. This statement was reported in a cable from the American Ambassador in France, William G. Sharp, to Lansing, 31 January 1918, in *Foreign Relations, 1918*, Supplement 1, I, 64-65. Cf. Pershing, *My Experiences,* I, 309-310.

27. The entire statement is in *U. S. Army in World War,* II, 187.

28. Lloyd George, *War Memoirs,* V, 420. The six-division agreement is printed in *ibid.*, 419-420. Bliss reported that Lloyd George signed the agreement unhesitatingly. Bliss to Baker, 2 February 1918, Bliss Papers.

29. See the account of his interview with Sir William Wiseman, 3 February 1918, in Baker, *Life and Letters,* VII, 520-521.

30. This message is in a cable from the Adjutant General (McCain) to Pershing, 4 February 1918, printed in *U. S. Army in World War,* III, 40.

31. Bliss to Baker, 2 February 1918, Bliss Papers.

32. See Pershing, *My Experiences,* I, 273-276; *U. S. Army in World War,* II, 210-214.

33. For the Lloyd George message, 28 March 1918, see *Foreign Relations, 1918*, Supplement 1, I, 180-182. Baker's attitude is related in Pershing, *My Experiences,* I, 356-357.

34. *Intimate Papers,* III, 437-439.

35. *Ibid.*, 441-442; Pershing, *My Experiences,* I, 358.

36. Minutes of the twenty-fourth meeting of the military representatives, 27 March 1918, SWC-WDA. Pershing left a memorandum summarizing his views. Pershing Memorandum on Amalgamation, 27 March 1918, Bliss Papers.

37. The joint note included the following points: "The Military Representatives are of opinion that it is highly desirable that the American Government should assist the Allied Armies as soon as possible, by permitting, in principle, the temporary service of American units in Allied army corps and divisions. . . . The units so temporarily employed must eventually be returned to the American Army. . . . The Military Representatives are of opinion that, for the present time . . . only American infantry and machine-gun units, organised as the Government may decide, be brought to France, and that all agreements or conventions hitherto made in conflict with this decision be modified accordingly." Joint Note No. 18, "Utilization of American Manpower," 27 March 1918, SWC-WDA. Reprinted in Lloyd George, *War Memoirs*, V, 424-425, and *U. S. Army in World War*, II, 257-258.

38. This interpretation is offered in Shumate, "The Allied Supreme War Council," 839.

39. Baker to Adjutant General, 28 March 1918, SWC-WDA. This message is reprinted in part in *U. S. Army in World War*, II, 261-262. See also Pershing, *My Experiences*, I, 360-362. Baker also dispatched a personal cable to President Wilson, 28 March 1918, explaining his suggestions. *Foreign Relations, 1918*, Supplement 1, I, 177-178.

40. Wilson's cable of 29 March 1918 is in *U. S. Army in World War*, II, 264. Colonel House wrote to his son-in-law, Gordon Auchincloss, indicating approval of this technique. House to Auchincloss, 27 March 1918, House Papers.

41. The British knew that Joint Note No. 18 applied only to the disposition of the six divisions whose shipment had been arranged in January and February 1918. This wave of combat troops would be followed immediately by their supporting units. See the British liaison officer's report to the British War Office from Pershing's G.H.Q. in *U. S. Army in World War*, III, 75-76.

42. See the message of Lloyd George to Lord Reading, 2 April 1918, in *ibid.*, 77-78.

43. Bliss had been informed of this project by the British Section at Versailles. He forwarded the information to Secretary of War Baker with the following indorsement: "I have carefully considered the Prime Minister's despatch and I fully concur in the action recommended by him to be taken by the American authori-

ties." Secretary of the British Section to Bliss, 30 March 1918, Bliss Papers.

44. These messages are in *U. S. Army in World War,* II, 278-279, 281-282. Pershing reacted immediately, writing to Baker on 5 April 1918: "There seems to me to be a real danger of the British political world allowing itself to be lulled into inaction upon the theory that the Americans are in a position to meet all possible contingencies." Pershing to Baker, 5 April 1918, Pershing Papers. See also Pershing, *My Experiences,* I, 386-387.

45. The President's message to Baker, 6 April 1918, is in *U. S. Army in World War,* III, 81.

46. Paraphrases of cables from Balfour to Reading, 8 April 1918, and Reading to Lloyd George, 10 April 1918, House Papers. Pershing and Baker, meeting with British officials on 7 April 1918, would discuss only the shipment and temporary amalgamation of 60,000 infantry troops during April. *U. S. Army in World War,* II, 286-288.

47. Pershing, *My Experiences,* I, 383-384.

48. For the evolution of this scheme and the justification for it, see *U. S. Army in World War,* II, 283-285, 290-294. The British immediately recognized the plan for what it was. See Lloyd George to Reading, 7 April 1918, in *ibid.,* III, 85-86. This cable intimated that Bliss and Baker tended to favor the British view. It provided an opportunity to stress the seeming conflict in American thinking.

49. House to Wilson, 9 April 1918, Wilson Papers.

50. Bliss to Baker, 10 April 1918, Bliss Papers.

51. See Foch's comment that it would be criminal to count on American support during the great battles because the United States was not moving troops to Europe as fast as anticipated. *U. S. Army in World War,* II, 322. Foch thought the American plans "too ineffective for words" and urged his government to press for their alteration. *Ibid.,* 338. At this time Pershing actually pressed Foch to allow him to form an American corps for the purpose of conducting independent operations. Pershing, *My Experiences,* I, 395. Bliss continued to press his views on the War Department. Bliss to March, 20 April 1918, SWC-WDA. This message is partially reproduced in *U. S. Army in World War,* II, 333.

52. This agreement, made on 21 April 1918, was reported by Reading to Lloyd George on the same date. *U. S. Army in World War,* II, 336-337. On 19 April General Pershing had agreed to place 60,000 troops with the British army during April and had deferred further arrangements to a later date. The War Department arrange-

ment far exceeded Pershing's commitments. Pershing's talks are summarized in *ibid.*, 329-330. Lloyd George's action is noted in Palmer, *Baker,* II, 169.

53. For the text of the Pershing-Milner Agreement, see *U. S. Army in World War,* III, 91-92. Pershing recounts these negotiations in his *My Experiences,* II, 5-9. He clearly implies that the President was unduly influenced by the capable Lord Reading and inveighs against the Baker-Reading arrangements as unhealthy precedents interfering with his determination to build a "balanced force."

54. For a report of the Pershing-Foch consultation, 25 April 1918, see *U. S. Army in World War,* II, 348-350. Pershing gives his views in *My Experiences,* II, 10-13.

55. *Ibid.*, 15-16. Pershing now had to deal with the dogmatic General Peyton C. March, Chief of Staff, who was not disposed to be ordered about by a theater commander. The best account of American mobilization during World War I is Kreidberg and Henry, *Military Mobilization in U. S. Army,* 175-376, which carefully traces the evolution of American plans under the impact of amalgamation.

56. Baker to Wilson, 29 April 1918, Baker Papers.

57. Baker to Bliss, 29 April 1918, quoted in Palmer, *Baker,* II, 169.

58. The notes of this gathering are in *U. S. Army in World War,* II, 355-356.

59. Minutes of the first meeting of the fifth session of the Supreme War Council, 1 May 1918, SWC-WDA. This debate is printed in *U. S. Army in World War,* II, 361-365. Note Pershing's account in *My Experiences,* II, 30-34.

60. Minutes of the third meeting of the fifth session of the Supreme War Council, 2 May 1918, SWC-WDA. The relevant portions are printed in *U. S. Army in World War,* II, 366-371. See also Maurice, *Lessons of Allied Co-operation,* 54. The text of the "Resolution regarding the co-operation of the American Army" is printed in *U. S. Army in World War,* II, 373-374.

61. The French recognized that General Pershing, in the future, would be even more difficult in connection with amalgamation. See the report of General Raguenau, Chief of the French Mission at Pershing's G.H.Q., 7 May 1918, in *ibid.*, 387-389.

62. Baker to Wilson, 4 May 1918, Baker Papers; Wilson to Baker, 6 May 1918, Baker Papers.

63. Baker to Bliss, 7 May 1918, Bliss Papers.

64. Bliss to Baker, 11 May 1918, Bliss Papers.

65. Baker to Wilson, 10 May 1918, Baker Papers.

66. The cable, dated 11 May 1918, is in *U. S. Army in World War,* II, 399.

67. See Pershing's cable of 15 May 1918, in *ibid.,* 403-404.

68. Wiseman to House, 11 May 1918, House Papers.

69. House to Wilson, 12 May 1918, House Papers.

70. House to Wilson, 20 May 1918, Wilson Papers. See also *Intimate Papers,* III, 446-447.

71. House to Wilson, 26 May 1918, House Papers.

72. See the text of the arrangement made with General Pétain, 19 May 1918, in *U. S. Army in World War,* II, 413-414. Pershing comments on this subject in his *My Experiences,* II, 53-54. Some American units actually followed this cycle. See the movements of the American Twenty-Eighth Division (National Guard) as listed in Historical Section, Army War College, *Order of Battle of the United States Land Forces in the World War; Divisions* (Washington, 1931), 140-151.

73. The American notes of this conference are in *U. S. Army in World War,* II, 438-441. See also Pershing, *My Experiences,* II, 71-78; Maurice, *Lessons of Allied Co-operation,* 150-151.

74. Minutes of the second meeting of the sixth session of the Supreme War Council, 2 June 1918, SWC-WDA.

75. "Resolution in Regard to American Shipping," passed by the Supreme War Council on 2 June 1918, SWC-WDA.

76. Pershing recognized the gravity of the situation and urged an increase in the American effort. He disagreed with the European leaders concerning the employment of American troops, but not with the Allied insistence on the need for them. See his message to March and Baker, 3 June 1918, in *U. S. Army in World War,* II, 449-450.

77. House to Wilson, 3 June 1918, House Papers.

78. In a letter to the President, Baker strongly defended Pershing's policy of pressing for an early establishment of an independent American army, citing increasing evidence of European debility as justification. Baker to Wilson, 5 June 1918, Wilson Papers.

79. Baker to Wilson, 8 June 1918, Baker Papers. The President's letter which evoked Baker's comments is Wilson to Baker, 7 June 1918, Baker Papers. Colonel House consulted General March concerning Pershing's capacity for diplomatic negotiations. March was extremely critical. "He ought not to be allowed to undertake diplomatic work of any kind. . . . He was peculiarly unfitted for it."

March, *Nation at War,* 194-195. Pershing's account of this episode is in his *My Experiences,* II, 179-191.

80. Baker to Pershing, 6 July 1918, Pershing Papers.

81. Pershing to Baker, 28 July 1918, Pershing Papers.

82. March to Bliss, 24 June 1918, SWC-WDA.

83. See the debate of the shipping requirements on 2 July 1918 during the first meeting of the seventh session of the Supreme War Council, *U. S. Army in World War,* II, 499-500. See also Maurice, *Lessons of Allied Co-operation,* 154-155.

84. Details of the American manpower program are in Kreidberg and Henry, *Military Mobilization in U. S. Army,* 302-306. For the establishment of the First Army see Pershing, *My Experiences,* II, 175, 216-218. Pershing believed the new mobilization plan was essential in order to sustain European morale. Pershing to Baker, 28 July 1918, Pershing Papers.

85. The British reluctance to provide tonnage for the eighty-division program particularly irritated American leaders. The President thought this hesitance "characteristic." Baker, *Life and Letters,* VIII, 328. Bliss believed the British still thought they could trade ships for troops. Bliss to Baker, 22 August 1918, Wilson Papers.

86. Lord Reading talked to Pershing during a visit to Europe and later wrote to Wiseman telling him that Pershing was just as stubborn as ever concerning amalgamation. He noted that Pershing might attempt to thwart Foch on some point and that his tendency to insubordination ought to be told to Colonel House and "probably" to the President. Reading to Wiseman, 12 September 1918, House Papers.

87. The quick withdrawal of the American army from Europe as soon as possible after the armistice seems to strengthen the view that having troops in Europe in order to influence the peace conference was not a really basic concept of American policy, especially after the success of Colonel House in negotiating inter-Allied acceptance of the Fourteen Points and associated statements at the pre-armistice conference in Paris just before the war ended. This subject is discussed at length in Chapter 8.

88. For an example of this kind of justification, see Thomas C. Lonergan, *It Might Have Been Lost* (New York, 1929).

CHAPTER 6: *Intervention in Russia*

1. An account of the negotiations in Paris is in George F. Kennan, *Soviet-American Relations, 1917-1920,* I, *Russia Leaves the War* (Princeton, 1956), 131-140. Colonel House summed up the

results in House to Wilson, 2 December 1917, Wilson Papers.

2. House to Wilson, 1 December 1917, House Papers.

3. Joint Note No. 5, "The Situation in Russia," 24 December 1917, SWC-WDA. The British War Cabinet followed this action with a policy statement indicating their desire to avoid a rupture with the Bolsheviks and accepting in principle the formula of "no indemnities, no annexations." This action, taken on 26 December 1917, is discussed by Shumate, "The Allied Supreme War Council," 237-238.

4. Specialists on intervention in Russia offer several causal interpretations. John A. White stresses economic motives as the basis for intervention. He believes the German and Japanese efforts to control Siberia forced the Allies to take actions against their rivals. John A. White, *The Siberian Intervention* (Princeton, 1953), 15, 218. This perspective does not specifically call attention to the anti-Bolshevik motivations which influenced the Allies. General Graves, the commanding general of the American expedition which landed in Siberia in August 1918, stresses anti-Bolshevik sentiments. William S. Graves, *America's Siberian Adventure: 1918-1920* (New York, 1931), 69. Graves' opinions are based on his experiences after August 1918, when anti-Bolshevik feeling boiled to the surface. Note the opinion of General Bliss: "The original idea was not primarily to initiate a war against Bolshevism as such but was merely to bring about a renewal of a Russian threat against East Germany." "Final Report" of General Bliss, SWC-WDA. The early British negotiations with the Bolsheviks, conducted through Bruce Lockhart, do not indicate an inflexible ideological opposition to the new Russian regime, at least in the period prior to the "terror." See R. H. Bruce Lockhart, *British Agent* (New York, 1933).

5. Kennan, *Soviet-American Relations*, I, 208-215. When Lansing heard of the French proposal he called in Sato, the Japanese Ambassador, who confirmed the rumors. *Foreign Relations, 1918, Russia,* II, 13.

6. See message from the Acting Foreign Secretary to the British Ambassador, Lord Cecil to Spring Rice, 1 January 1918, Wilson Papers.

7. The text of the message is in *Foreign Relations, 1918, Russia,* II, 20-21.

8. *Ibid.*, 28-29. Ambassador Morris in Tokyo thought the Japanese would seize any opportunity to intervene. *Ibid.*, 23-27.

9. For these developments, see *ibid.*, 35-36, 38, 41-43, 45-46.

10. Balfour to House, 30 January 1918, House Papers.

11. House to Wilson, 2 February 1918, Wilson Papers.

12. Balfour to House, 8 February 1918, and House to Balfour, 14 February 1918, House Papers.

13. House to Wilson, 2 February 1918, Wilson Papers.

14. Bliss to permanent military representatives, 15 February 1918, Bliss Papers.

15. Minutes of the seventeenth meeting of the military representatives, 18 February 1918, SWC-WDA.

16. Joint Note No. 16, "Japanese Intervention in Siberia," 19 February 1918, SWC-WDA.

17. Bliss to Lansing, Baker, and March, 19 February 1918, SWC-WDA. Bliss' recognition of the complexities of the Russian question is reflected in Bliss to March, 20 February 1918, Bliss Papers. He thought the Japanese might not withdraw when requested and that a Japanese-German coalition was a distinct possibility. He thought both the British and the French were moved partially by a desire to strengthen anti-Bolshevik factions in Russia.

18. Bliss to Baker, 25 February 1918, SWC-WDA. Bliss was obviously torn between his low estimate of military prospects in Siberia and the pro-interventionist pressure being exerted by the Allies.

19. Bliss to permanent military representatives, 26 February 1918, Bliss Papers.

20. Judson to Baker (Memorandum on Russia), 26 February 1918, Wilson Papers; Judson to Baker (Supplementary Memorandum on Russia), 4 March 1918, Wilson Papers.

21. *Foreign Relations, 1918, Russia,* II, 53-54.

22. See the opinion of Ambassador Sharp concerning the French attitude. *Ibid.,* 50-52, 58-60. General Pershing was informed of the French fear of German territorial aggrandizement in Russia. "E. R." (unidentified) to Pershing, 28 February 1918, Pershing Papers. Lord Reading presented a formal British request for intervention as far west as Cheliabinsk, a communications center just east of the Ural Mountains. Balfour to Reading, 26 February 1918, Wilson Papers. Ambassador Morris reported from Tokyo that the Japanese opposed further delays and might take unilateral action, provided the British and French approved, without waiting for American acquiescence. *Foreign Relations, 1918, Russia,* II, 56.

23. The activities of Americans in Russia during the spring and summer of 1918 are recounted in George F. Kennan, *Soviet-American Relations, 1917-1920,* II, *The Decision to Intervene* (Princeton, 1958).

24. Diary, 2 January 1918, House Papers.

25. See Lansing to Wilson, 2 February 1918, and Memorandum on Russia by Lansing, 6 January 1918, Wilson Papers.

26. Lansing, *War Memoirs*, 341.

27. Wilson, *Public Papers: War and Peace*, I, 159-160. Kennan stresses House's influence on the President in connection with the drafting of this portion of the speech. Kennan, *Soviet-American Relations*, I, 257.

28. Quoted in *ibid.*, 478.

29. Kennan argues that House originally concurred in the policy projected in the draft note to Japan but changed his mind later. *Ibid., loc. cit.*

30. Memorandum on Intervention by William C. Bullitt, 2 March 1918, Wilson Papers.

31. Diary, 3 March 1918, House Papers.

32. House to Wilson, 3 March 1918, Wilson Papers. House wrote to Balfour the next day, expressing somewhat similar sentiments. House to Balfour, 4 March 1918, House Papers. Balfour's reply reflected his desire for intervention despite the force of House's argument. Balfour to House, 6 March 1918, Wilson Papers.

33. The note of 5 March 1918 is in *Foreign Relations, 1918, Russia*, II, 67-68.

34. This episode is related in Kennan, *Soviet-American Relations*, I, 471-485. Kennan believes the American assumption that the Japanese intended to intervene unilaterally was an error.

35. Kennan implies this interpretation in *ibid.*, II, 404.

36. A summary of the Brest-Litovsk negotiations is in Robert D. Warth, *The Allies and the Russian Revolution* (Durham, 1954), 196-241. See also White, *The Siberian Intervention*, 222.

37. Baker, *Life and Letters*, VIII, 21.

38. *Foreign Relations, 1918, Russia*, II, 81-82. The British continued to advocate intervention, but apparently they recognized that it could not be accomplished without American aid. Balfour to Wilson, 18 March 1918, Wilson Papers.

39. On 12 March French Ambassador Jules Jusserand pressed Lansing for a reconsideration of American policy. The Secretary refused to take action. *Foreign Relations, 1918, Russia*, II, 75-77, 80. A personal letter to the President failed to elicit a satisfactory response. Jusserand to Wilson, 17 March 1918, Wilson Papers.

40. Minutes of the second meeting of the fourth session of the Supreme War Council, 14 March 1918, SWC-WDA.

41. The minutes of the political conference, 15 March 1918, are in SWC-WDA. See also Frazier's report in W. H. Page to Lansing, 16 March 1918, House Papers.

42. Joint Report of the miltary and naval representatives, 23 March 1918, SWC-WDA. In a separate gathering on the same day the military representatives decided not to favor the use of troops in Russia if they were needed in France. Minutes of the twenty-second meeting of the military representatives, 23 March 1918, SWC-WDA.

43. This fear is reported in Bliss to March, 10 April 1918, Bliss Papers. The War Department thought enough of the situation to order an investigation into the strength of the British army in India. *U. S. Army in World War,* II, 345.

44. Paper by General H. W. Studd, British Section, Supreme War Council (undated), "Allied Intervention in Russia. . ." in SWC-WDA. The fear of German penetration into south Asia continued to worry the British. Balfour to Reading (paraphrase), 15 April 1918, Wilson Papers. Lloyd George feared the Germans might establish an impregnable line along the Rhine and turn to a wholesale exploitation of the East, realizing that gains could not be made in Western Europe. Lloyd George, *War Memoirs,* VI, 167.

45. Sharp to Lansing, 11 April 1918, Wilson Papers.

46. White, *The Siberian Intervention,* 233-236; Graves, *America's Siberian Adventure,* 24-26.

47. Joint Note No. 20, "The Situation in the Eastern Theatre," 8 April 1918, SWC-WDA.

48. See the unsigned memorandum on Russia prepared by the War Department for the President and forwarded to him on 11 October 1917, Wilson Papers. This paper concluded that Russia should be considered a possible theater only if it became the sole field open to American military activity by reason of submarine warfare.

49. "Final Report" of General Bliss, SWC-WDA. See also the minutes of the twenty-fifth meeting of the permanent military representatives, 8 April 1918, SWC-WDA. Bliss discussed the new British motivations in Bliss to March, 10 April 1918, SWC-WDA. He attributed Joint Note No. 20 to British fears that they might have to divert a large body of troops to India in order to quell native uprisings. Bliss to Lansing, Baker, and March, 12 April 1918, SWC-WDA.

50. Joint Note No. 25, "Transportation of Czech Troops from Russia," 27 April 1918, SWC-WDA. The discussion of the note by the military representatives indicates that they thought Murmansk rather than Vladivostok was the best route out of Russia for the Czech

Legion. Minutes of the twenty-seventh meeting of the permanent military representatives, 27 April 1918, SWC-WDA.

51. Minutes of the second and third meetings of the fifth session of the Supreme War Council, 2 May 1918, SWC-WDA.

52. Bliss to Baker, 26 May 1918, SWC-WDA.

53. March to Bliss, 28 May 1918, SWC-WDA.

54. *Foreign Relations, 1918, Russia,* II, 182.

55. Shumate, "The Allied Supreme War Council," 727. A good summary of the Czech uprising is in White, *The Siberian Intervention,* 236-255. See also Kennan, *Soviet-American Relations,* II, 277-295.

56. Lansing to Wilson, 11 May 1918, Wilson Papers. See also White, *The Siberian Intervention,* 229.

57. Baker, *Life and Letters,* VIII, 153. The American Consul at Murmansk, Felix Cole, did not think intervention was justifiable. He thought the terrain would frustrate military activity and that intervention would strengthen the tie between Russia and Germany. If intervention took place, he believed the United States would "lose that moral superiority over Germany which is a tower of strength to us everywhere, because we shall have descended to using Germany's own weapons; namely, intervention and force." This argument paralleled the views of Colonel House which had been so influential in March. *Foreign Relations, 1918, Russia,* II, 477-484.

58. For a British proposal to send a joint Anglo-American force to Murmansk, see *ibid.*, 476. Ambassador David Francis called for intervention at Murmansk. *Ibid.*, 474. Bliss was notified of the change in American policy in March to Bliss, 28 May 1918, SWC-WDA.

59. Bliss to permanent military representatives, 1 June 1918, Bliss Papers.

60. Joint Note No. 31, "Allied Intervention at Russian Allied Ports [Murmansk and Archangel]," 3 June 1918, SWC-WDA.

61. Minutes of the sixth session of the Supreme War Council, 1-3 June 1918, SWC-WDA.

62. The President's message concerning Foch is in *Foreign Relations, 1918, Russia,* II, 484-485. For the naval movement see *ibid.*, 487.

63. Baker to Bliss, 9 June 1918, Baker Papers. In this message Baker indicated that the War Department opposed the Murmansk proposal. He asked Bliss to express his views, by implication seeking reasons why Bliss had signed Joint Note No. 31. Baker later asked Bliss to ascertain the views of Foch. Baker to Bliss, 15 June 1918,

SWC-WDA. Foch replied with an indorsement of the project for intervention in north Russia. Foch, *Memoirs*, 346-347.

64. Minutes of the third meeting of the sixth session of the Supreme War Council, SWC-WDA. See also the report of Arthur Frazier in *Foreign Relations, 1918, Russia*, II, 202-203.

65. Bliss to March, 24 June 1918, Bliss Papers.

66. March to Baker, 24 June 1918, Wilson Papers.

67. Bliss to Baker, 3 July 1918, Bliss Papers. The Japanese refusal to penetrate to Cheliabinsk enhanced American suspicions. The Japanese were not interested in western Siberia.

68. Memorandum to President Wilson, with resolution passed by the first meeting of the seventh session of the Supreme War Council, 2 July 1918, SWC-WDA.

69. Minutes of the seventh session of the Supreme War Council, 2-4 July 1918, SWC-WDA.

70. Baker, *Life and Letters*, VIII, 248. Permission to send the troops to Murmansk was given later in July. March to Bliss, 23 July 1918, SWC-WDA.

71. Basil Miles to Lansing, 1 July 1918, Wilson Papers; Baker to Wilson, 2 July 1918, Wilson Papers.

72. House thought Japan would cause serious trouble in the future if not given some freedom of action. House to Wilson, 6 July 1918, Wilson Papers.

73. March, *Nation at War*, 124-126. General March thought no real military opportunity existed in Siberia and that Japan would refuse to restrict her forces to the seven-thousand-man contingent envisioned by President Wilson.

74. Diary, 6 July 1918, Lansing Papers.

75. The President revealed his serious misgivings about intervention in Wilson to House, 8 July 1918, House Papers.

76. Baker wrote to Bliss at this time, reiterating his belief that intervention would vitiate the American effort in France. Palmer, *Baker*, II, 318. Bliss remained a staunch advocate of the western strategy, but his exposure to the currents of opinion at Versailles made him somewhat sensitive to the need to compromise with the Entente. Bliss to March, 10 July 1918, SWC-WDA. He approved nominal participation in the expedition to north Russia because "there will be an undercurrent of resentment if we do not take part." Bliss to Baker and March, 13 July 1918, SWC-WDA. In his introduction to General Graves' book, Baker gave his reasons for opposing intervention. Graves, *America's Siberian Adventure*, viii-ix. Later

he became somewhat more appreciative of the President's point of view. See his "Personal Observations about the North Russian and Siberian Expeditions," 11 November 1924, Baker Papers. See also the transcript of an interview of Baker by R. S. Baker, 6 April 1928, R. S. Baker Papers.

77. For accounts of conversations with Ishii, see Lansing to Wilson, 8 July 1918, and Lansing to Wilson, 10 July 1918, Wilson Papers. Lansing's tendency to favor the intervention might have resulted from his increasing feeling that Germany, frustrated in the West, might attempt a broad exploitation in the East. *Foreign Relations, 1918,* Supplement 1, I, 282. The Japanese sought to obtain the appointment of a Japanese general to command the Siberian expedition. Wilson finally agreed to this request. Roy W. Curry, *Woodrow Wilson and Far Eastern Policy, 1913-1921* (New York, 1957), 233.

78. For Lansing's report of Reading's irritation, see Lansing to Wilson, 9 July 1918, Wilson Papers. President Wilson revealed his distrust of Japanese intentions to Sir William Wiseman in a personal interview. Notes by Wiseman, 13 July 1918, House Papers. Some British observers were inclined to approve of the President's policy of restraint. See Murray to Wiseman, 16 July 1918, Wiseman Papers.

79. Baker later indicated that the President composed the *aide-mémoire*. Graves, *America's Siberian Adventure*, x.

80. The *aide-mémoire* is printed in *Foreign Relations, 1918, Russia*, II, 287-290. White is one of the few to emphasize the clearly non-interventionist nature of the *aide-mémoire*. White, *The Siberian Intervention*, 230-232.

81. This message is printed in *Foreign Relations, 1918, Russia*, II, 315-317. See Lloyd George's sarcastic comment on the President's policy in his *War Memoirs*, VI, 178-179.

82. The most recent work on the Siberian intervention is Betty S. Unterberger, *America's Siberian Expedition, 1918-1920: A Study of National Policy* (Durham, 1956). She agrees with White in assuming that "Wilson's basic and unpublicized reason for intervention was to restrain Japan from imperialistic adventures and to preserve the open door in Siberia and North Manchuria." *Ibid.*, 232. Future studies of intervention undoubtedly will adopt a broader causal interpretation, taking into account the immediate military and political situations, the President's burning desire for a just peace, the history of American policy in the Far East, and the necessities imposed by the importance of cooperating as much as possible with the Entente. Of great importance in the study of the background of intervention is George Kennan's recent study cited previously.

CHAPTER 7: *The Supreme War Council and the Macedonian Campaign*

1. House to Wilson, 23 June 1918, House Papers.

2. Bliss wanted to keep a careful record of the praises given American troops by Entente leaders. "There may be a tendency a year or so from now to minimize the credit which at the moment they gave to our troops." Bliss to Pershing, 6 July 1918, SWC-WDA. Earlier Bliss made the same suggestion to Secretary Baker. Bliss to Baker, 26 June 1918, Bliss Papers. The action is unimportant by itself, but it symbolizes the suspicion of European intentions in the minds of American leaders.

3. Lloyd George, *War Memoirs*, VI, 191-192.

4. See the British official history, *Military Operations, Macedonia: From the Spring of 1917 to the End of the War* (London, 1935), 321-322. A parallel volume in the French official history is *Les armées françaises dans la grande guerre*, Tome VII, Troisième Volume, *La campagne d'Orient, d'Avril 1918 á Décembre 1918* (Paris, 1934). See also the three volumes of accompanying documents. *Annexes–Troisième Volume* (Paris, 1934).

5. Shumate, "The Allied Supreme War Council," 17-18.

6. *Military Operations, Macedonia*, 73-76.

7. Callwell, *Sir Henry Wilson*, II, 113.

8. Minutes of the second meeting of the seventh session of the Supreme War Council, 3 July 1918, SWC-WDA. See also Callwell, *Sir Henry Wilson*, II, 113.

9. *Military Operations, Macedonia*, 105.

10. Note the comment of Sir Henry Wilson: "This (7th) meeting of the Supreme War Council was the angriest we have had, but I was very anxious that we should give the French clearly to understand that they were not going to take us over, body and bones, and take charge of every theatre. We have done this plainly—if a little, and unnecessarily, roughly." Callwell, *Sir Henry Wilson*, II, 113-114.

11. Blake, ed., *Private Papers of Douglas Haig*, 316.

12. Minutes of the seventh session of the Supreme War Council, 2-4 July 1918, SWC-WDA. Frazier's report on this session correctly identified the British purpose, to strengthen the Council, but he did not seem to realize that the British sought thereby to lessen the prestige of France. Frazier to House, 6 July 1918, House Papers.

13. Foch, *Memoirs*, 355-356.

14. Frazier to House, 10 July and 25 July 1918, House Papers.

15. "The Functions of the Versailles Organization," 16 July 1918, carbon copy from files of the British Section, Supreme War Council, House Papers. This episode and its ramifications are discussed at length in Shumate, "The Allied Supreme War Council," 857-885.

16. Baker to Bliss, 1 July 1918, SWC-WDA.

17. Lochridge, Embick, Browning, and Ward to Bliss, 9 July 1918, SWC-WDA.

18. Bliss to permanent military representatives, 9 July 1918, Bliss Papers.

19. Bliss to Baker, 17 July 1918, Bliss Papers.

20. Minutes of the forty-first meeting of the permanent military representatives, 29 July 1918, SWC-WDA.

21. *Military Operations, Macedonia,* 110-111. This resolution was approved on 3 August 1918. Bliss' action incurred the wrath of the author who prepared the British official history of the Macedonian campaign.

22. *Ibid.*, 111-112.

23. *Ibid.*, 203-204.

24. Lloyd George makes this judgment in his *War Memoirs,* VI, 198-200.

25. Bliss to Baker, 22 July 1918, Bliss Papers.

26. Bliss to March, 5 August 1918, Bliss Papers.

27. *Ibid.*

28. Bliss to Baker, 9 August 1918, Bliss Papers. (The copy in the Wilson Papers is dated 7 August 1918.)

29. Bliss to Baker, 14 August 1918, printed in *U.S. Army in World War*, II, 571-573.

30. Baker, *Life and Letters,* VIII, 360.

31. For a discussion of this program, see Kreidberg and Henry, *Military Mobilization in the United States Army,* 302-309.

32. Bliss to Baker, 22 August 1918, Wilson Papers.

33. Baker to Wilson, 23 August 1918, Wilson Papers. Baker interpreted the Bliss messages as requests for the President to make a personal representation to Foch.

34. House to Wilson, 3 September 1918, Wilson Papers.

35. Willert, *Road to Safety,* 156-157; *Intimate Papers,* IV, 61-63; Baker, *Life and Letters,* VIII, 341-342.

36. *Ibid.*, 364-365, 381; *Foreign Relations, 1918*, Supplement

1, I, 518-519, 524. See also the letter from Hurley to the President which pointed out certain British efforts along these lines. Hurley to Wilson, 23 September 1918, Wilson Papers.

37. Wilson to Hurley, 29 August 1918, Wilson Papers.

38. Joint Note No. 37, "General Military Policy of the Allies for the Autumn of 1918 and for the Year 1919," 10 September 1918, SWC-WDA.

39. Letters from Bliss to the War Department reveal his increasing interest in and distrust of Entente motives in Russia and Macedonia. He was also critical of the Italian effort to revive the offensive against Austria. See Bliss to March, 7-12-16-18 September 1918, and Bliss to Baker, 3 October 1918, SWC-WDA.

40. Bliss to House, 12 September 1918, House Papers.

41. Bliss to Baker, 3 October 1918, SWC-WDA.

42. Scott, *War Aims and Peace Proposals*, 405-409.

43. See Ambassador Sharp's report on changing European moods. Sharp to Wilson, 16 September 1918, Wilson Papers.

44. Scott, *War Aims and Peace Proposals*, 396.

45. For a comment by Balfour, see *ibid.*, 389-396. The Italian response is in *ibid.*, 397.

46. The collapse of Bulgaria appears to have stimulated considerable dissension among the Allied and Associated Powers. The surrender came on 29 September through the G.H.Q. of General Franchet d'Espérey, the commander in the theater. *Ibid.*, 398, 405-406. Bulgaria attempted to enlist the good offices of President Wilson, and the latter decided to accept the invitation. Bulgaria, however, had to accept the severe terms imposed by D'Espérey before the President could take action. Baker, *Life and Letters*, VIII, 425, 428-430, 434-435; *Intimate Papers*, IV, 59-60. After news of the surrender arrived in Washington, the President gave notice to the Entente Powers that the Bulgarian peace treaty could not be considered apart from the general settlement, thus giving notice that he would exercise his powerful influence in connection with all aspects of the peace settlement. *Foreign Affairs, 1918*, Supplement 1, I, 334. Sir Henry Wilson's diary reflects his irritation as evidence of the President's intentions came to him. Callwell, *Sir Henry Wilson*, II, 130-131.

47. Scott, *War Aims and Peace Proposals*, 399-405.

48. See the commentary on this speech in *Intimate Papers*, IV, 69-70.

49. Scott, *War Aims and Peace Proposals*, 418-419. President

Wilson received information indicating that the Allies intended to sidetrack the Fourteen Points and his other war aims if they could manage it. For example, see Hollis to Wilson, 2 October 1918, Wilson Papers.

CHAPTER 8: *The Pre-Armistice Negotiations*

1. The note is in Scott, *War Aims and Peace Proposals*, 409-414. The course of German policy is illustrated with documents in James B. Scott, ed., *Preliminary History of the Armistice: Official Documents Published by the German National Chancellery by Order of the Ministry of State* (New York, 1924), 5-48.

2. Scott, *War Aims and Peace Proposals*, 418-419. Colonel House had urged the President to adopt a policy of delay while not rejecting the note out of hand. *Intimate Papers*, IV, 75-76.

3. Note the comment by Sir Henry Wilson in his diary entry for 6 October 1918: "Lloyd George took the line that we pandered too much to President Wilson. Bob [Lord Cecil] and Bonar Law were all in favor of conciliating him. I agree with Lloyd George, and am certain that a few good home truths would do the President good." Callwell, *Sir Henry Wilson*, II, 134. See also *ibid.*, 139-141. Colonel House thought the Allies wanted President Wilson to continue his discussions with the Central Powers, but he was clearly wrong. *Intimate Papers*, IV, 75-76.

4. "Principles Submitted by a Conference of Prime Ministers to a Joint Meeting of the Military and Naval Representatives," 7 October 1918, SWC-WDA.

5. "Joint Resolution Regarding Conditions of an Armistice with Germany and Austria-Hungary," in minutes of the joint meeting of the military and naval representatives, 8 October 1918, SWC-WDA.

6. W. B. Wallace to Secretary, British Section of the Supreme War Council, 16 October 1918, SWC-WDA. Admiral Sims forwarded the naval terms to Washington but Secretary Daniels withheld instructions until consultations were held. Baker, *Life and Letters*, VIII, 457-458, 463-464, 465.

7. Bliss to Baker, 9 October 1918, Bliss Papers. This point of view also is reflected in Bliss to March, 14 October 1918, Wilson Papers; Bliss to Hamilton Holt, 10 October 1918, House Papers.

8. Tumulty to Wilson, 10 October 1918, Wilson Papers.

9. Bliss to March, 14 October 1918, SWC-WDA.

10. Callwell, *Sir Henry Wilson*, II, 135. Frazier reported a conversation with Lloyd George in which the latter expressed disagreement with certain of the Fourteen Points, in particular freedom of the seas. The Prime Minister said that Clemenceau agreed with him. *Foreign Relations, 1918*, Supplement 1, I, 351-352. Frazier also gave the contents of the message requesting the dispatch of an American delegate to the pre-armistice negotiations, a report included in Sharp to Lansing, 9 October 1918, House Papers.

11. Frazier to Lansing, 9 October 1918, Wilson Papers. The message is printed in *Foreign Relations, 1918*, Supplement 1, I, 353.

12. Paraphrase of cable, Balfour to Barclay, 13 October 1918, Wilson Papers. Sir Henry Wilson recorded the irritation of the British government in his diary on 13 October: "As regards Wilson, we agreed that we would wire to say he must make it clear to the Boches that his 14 points (with which we do not agree) were not a basis for an armistice, which is what the Boche pretend they are. . . . Everyone angry and contemptuous of Wilson." Callwell, *Sir Henry Wilson*, II, 136.

13. Scott, *War Aims and Peace Proposals*, 420-421.

14. *Ibid.*, 421-423; Baker, *Life and Letters*, VIII, 478; *Intimate Papers*, IV, 83-84.

15. Scott, *War Aims and Peace Proposals*, 428-429.

16. Scott, *War Aims and Peace Proposals*, 429-431; *Intimate Papers*, IV, 83-84. The evolution of German policy is traced in documents in Scott, *Preliminary History of the Armistice*, 49-107.

17. Baker, *Life and Letters*, VIII, 502.

18. Scott, *War Aims and Peace Proposals*, 434-436.

19. *Ibid.*, 438-439. The resignation of Ludendorff and the abdication of the Kaiser stemmed at least partially from the pressure exerted during this period by President Wilson.

20. *Ibid.*, 428-429, 440-441.

21. *Foreign Relations, 1918*, Supplement 1, I, 384.

22. Bliss to Baker, 23 October 1918, SWC-WDA.

23. Bliss to House (memorandum), 28 October 1918, House Papers.

24. Pershing, *My Experiences*, II, 359-363. For Haig's view see Cooper, *Haig*, II, 394; Blake, ed., *Private Papers of Douglas Haig*, 336.

25. Printed in *Intimate Papers*, IV, 143-145.

26. Baker, *Life and Letters,* VIII, 515-516; Pershing, *My Experiences,* II, 362.

27. Baker, *Life and Letters,* VIII, 521-522; Pershing, *My Experiences,* II, 362.

28. Wilson to House, 28 October 1918, Wilson Papers. For a discussion of this message, somewhat altered in the process of decoding when it arrived in Paris, see W. Stull Holt, "What Wilson Sent and What House Received; Or Scholars Ought to Check Carefully," *The American Historical Review* (April, 1960), LXV, 569-571.

29. Pershing to the Supreme War Council, 30 October 1918, Wilson Papers; Pershing, *My Experiences,* II, 366-367.

30. Baker to Wilson, 31 October 1918, Wilson Papers.

31. Pershing, *My Experiences,* II, 368.

32. Baker to Wilson, 5 November 1918, and Wilson to Baker, 7 November 1918, Baker Papers. Clemenceau had apparently attempted to procure Foch's support in an effort to force the dismissal of General Pershing just prior to the pre-armistice discussions. Foch, *Memoirs,* 434-436.

33. *Foreign Relations, 1918,* Supplement 1, I, 394-395.

34. Maurice, *Lessons of Allied Co-operation,* 168-169.

35. *Ibid., loc. cit.*

36. Sims to House and Benson, 29 October 1918, House Papers.

37. Baker, *Life and Letters,* VIII, 482.

38. *Foreign Relations, 1918,* Supplement 1, I, 525-527.

39. *Ibid.,* 445-447, 472. House raised the question of Bolshevism several times at Paris. *Intimate Papers,* IV, 118-119, 139. The Germans were obsessed with the threat of a Bolshevik uprising. See Scott, *Preliminary History of the Armistice,* 51, 53-54, 56, 72-73, 79-80. General Bliss was also concerned about Bolshevism in Germany, but he did not think it an argument in favor of a moderate armistice. He thought the army would be just as susceptible to Bolshevik propaganda as others in Germany. The future proved him right. Bliss to Baker, 10 November 1918, Bliss Papers.

40. *Intimate Papers,* IV, 119-124, 147; Pershing, *My Experiences,* IV, 368-369.

41. *Intimate Papers,* IV, 126-136.

42. Quoted from House's diary in *ibid.,* 135-136.

43. The Allies did not object *in toto* to the Fourteen Points. Each nation tended to oppose particular points which appeared to

threaten the national interest. The speech on war aims delivered by Lloyd George on 5 January 1918, while more general in character than the President's speech of 8 January, indicates that the British and American positions were relatively close. The speech of Lloyd George is quoted in full in his *War Memoirs*, V, 63-73.

44. The President felt that the principles in the Fourteen Points should remain general and that specific applications, in particular the league, should develop out of actual experience. Wilson to House, 22 March 1918, House Papers.

45. Maurice, *Lessons of Allied Co-operation*, 166-167; *Intimate Papers*, IV, 161-162. For British objections to the Fourteen Points during this period, see *Foreign Relations, 1918*, Supplement 1, I, 365-367. Brand Whitlock, the Ambassador to Belgium, reported the Belgian desire to be consulted on the armistice. *Ibid.*, 344. Thomas N. Page, the Ambassador to Italy, reported Italian fears. *Ibid.*, 375-376.

46. *Intimate Papers*, IV, 162-164.

47. House to Lansing, 29 October 1918, House Papers.

48. *Intimate Papers*, IV, 164-167.

49. *Foreign Relations, 1918*, Supplement 1, I, 424.

50. House to Lansing, 29 October 1918, House Papers. The Cobb-Lippmann Memorandum is printed in *Intimate Papers*, IV, 192-200. See also *ibid.*, 152-154.

51. Wilson to House, 29 October 1918, Wilson Papers. The President followed this message with another, this one dealing with freedom of the seas and the league. It further strengthened House's position. *Foreign Relations, 1918*, Supplement 1, I, 523.

52. House to Wilson, 30 October 1918, House Papers.

53. House to Lansing for Wilson, 30 October 1918, House Papers.

54. *Intimate Papers*, IV, 170-174.

55. House to Lansing for Wilson, 30 October 1918, House Papers.

56. House to Wilson, 31 October 1918, House Papers.

57. *Foreign Relations, 1918*, Supplement 1, I, 427-428.

58. *Ibid.*, 455-457.

59. Wilson to House, 3 November 1918, Wilson Papers.

60. Baker, *Life and Letters*, VIII, 543.

61. The text of the Pre-Armistice Agreement follows: "The Allied Governments have given careful consideration to the corre-

spondence which [has] passed between the President of the United States and the German Government. Subject to the qualifications which follow they declare their willingness to make peace with the Government of Germany on the terms of peace laid down in the President's address to Congress of January 8, 1918, and the principles of settlement enunciated in his subsequent addresses [the Four Principles and the Five Particulars]. They must point out, however, that clause two, relating to what is usually described as the Freedom of the Seas, is open to various interpretations, some of which they could not accept. They must therefore reserve to themselves complete freedom on this subject when they enter the Peace Conference.

"Further, in the conditions of peace laid down in his address to Congress of January 8, 1918, the President declared that invaded territories must be restored as well as evacuated and freed. The Allied Governments feel that no doubt ought to be allowed to exist as to what this provision implies. By it they understand that compensation will be made by Germany for all damage done to the civilian population of the Allies and their property (by the forces of Germany) by the aggression of Germany, by land, by sea and from the air." This is the text transmitted in House to Wilson, 4 November 1918, House Papers.

62. House to Wilson, 5 November 1918, House Papers.

63. House to Wilson, 10 November 1918, House Papers.

Annotated Bibliography

I. *Sources*

A. Manuscript Sources

Baker, Newton D. Private Papers. Library of Congress, Washington, D.C.

As Secretary of War, Baker concerned himself primarily with mobilizing men and materials. He consciously deferred to his professional military associates in matters of strategy. His correspondence with President Wilson and General Bliss is of great importance in the study of inter-Allied cooperation. Baker often transmitted instructions to Bliss in the form of personal letters.

Baker, Ray Stannard. Private Papers. Library of Congress, Washington, D.C.

When preparing the authorized biography of President Wilson, Baker collected a great deal of information about the World War through personal interviews and correspondence with the leading Wilsonians. Some of this collection pertains to diplomacy, strategy, and inter-Allied consultation.

Bliss, General Tasker H. Private Papers. Library of Congress, Washington, D.C.

The American military representative's papers include considerable material concerning his assignment at Versailles. His correspondence with Baker and March is one of the most important sources of information about American activities at the Supreme War Council. The collection also includes copies of official documents issued by the Supreme War Council and the military representatives.

House, Edward M. Private Papers. Yale University Library, New Haven, Connecticut.

This collection throws much light on the role of the President's intimate friend. Much of it is included in the published memoirs of the Colonel edited by Charles Seymour, but much of the unpublished material is useful for the study of inter-Allied relationships. The correspondence between House and his informant in Paris, Arthur Hugh Frazier, is especially rewarding. The Colonel's manuscript diary is particularly valuable.

Lansing, Robert. Private Papers. Library of Congress, Washington, D.C.

Much of this collection has been published in the *Foreign Relations* series. Its value is limited because the wartime Secretary of State did not exercise much influence over the course of strategy and policy. President Wilson tended to be his own secretary of state.

Pershing, General John J. Private Papers. Library of Congress, Washington, D.C.

This collection is remarkably unrewarding for the study of inter-Allied cooperation. The General had little to do with the Supreme War Council except in connection with the dispute over amalgamation. Some light is cast on Pershing's relationships with the War Department.

Wilson, President Woodrow. Private Papers. Library of Congress, Washington, D.C.

The wartime President's papers are indispensable to any basic study dealing with the United States during World War I. The papers throw light on the President's diplomatic objectives, the nature of his influence on the formation of American strategy, and his attitude toward the Entente Powers. The President's letters to others are often unrewarding, but the letters sent to him often include important data. There is a chronological file of correspondence for the war years and another which includes correspondence with individuals.

Wiseman, Sir William. Private Papers. Yale University Library, New Haven, Connecticut.

These papers, not as yet arranged, give indications of British policy and of Wiseman's role as a liaison officer between House and the British government.

B. ARCHIVAL SOURCES.

Records of the Supreme War Council. State Department Records. National Archives, Washington, D.C.

This collection is limited. It contains copies of official documents issued by the Supreme War Council which General Bliss forwarded to Washington. Of interest is the correspondence between Arthur Hugh Frazier and various officials in the State Department, notably Gordon Auchincloss. The relative lack of significant material in this collection stems from the limited functions of the State Department during the administrations of President Wilson.

Records of the Supreme War Council. War Department Records. Record Group 120. American Expeditionary Forces. National Archives, Washington, D.C.

These records include much of the correspondence and official documents filed by General Bliss' staff. The collection is large and poorly organized. It is the principal source of information concerning the institutional characteristics of the Supreme War Council and the daily operations of the American Section. Much of General Bliss' correspondence is deposited in this collection. Perhaps because the American Section seems to have been understaffed, much that one would expect to find is not there.

C. Published Documents.

Hansard's Parliamentary Debates. House of Commons (Fifth Series), 1917-1918.

These debates are useful for Prime Minister Lloyd George's statements on inter-Allied matters. They also reflect British public opinion as understood by members of Parliament and the ministry.

Historical Section, Army War College, *Order of Battle of the United States Land Forces in the World War; Divisions.* Washington, 1931.

This work lists the movements of American troop units during World War I.

Papers Relating to the Foreign Relations of the United States.

The Lansing Papers. Vol. II, Washington, 1940.

1917. Supplement 2, *The World War.* Vol. II, Washington, 1932.

1918. Supplement 1, *The World War.* Vol. I, Washington, 1933.

1918. Russia. Vol. II, Washington, 1932.

The supplements for 1917 and 1918 conveniently collect

documents dealing specifically with the war. The special compilation of material on Russia is useful for the study of intervention in Bolshevik Russia. *The Lansing Papers* include the "Report" of General Bliss on the Supreme War Council.

Scott, James Brown, ed., *Official Statements of War Aims and Peace Proposals, December 1916 to November 1918.* Washington, 1921.

This collection includes commentaries by members of both the Allied and Associated Powers and the Central Powers.

————, ed., *Preliminary History of the Armistice: Official Documents Published by the German National Chancellery by Order of the Ministry of State.* New York, 1924.

These documents provide data on German policy prior to the Armistice of 11 November 1918.

Wilson, Woodrow, *The Public Papers of Woodrow Wilson.* Ray Stannard Baker and William E. Dodd, eds. 6 vols. New York, 1925-1927.

War and Peace: Presidential Messages, Addresses, and Public Papers (1917-1924). Vol. I. New York, 1927.

A useful source for the President's pronouncements on war aims during the conflict.

D. Official Military Histories

Der Weltkrieg: 1914-1918: Bearbeitet in Reichsarchiv. Kriegsgeschichtlichen Forschungsanstalt des Heeres. 14 vols. Berlin, 1925-1942.

The German official history concerns itself with Allied as well as German operations.

History of the Great War Based on Official Documents. Great Britain. Committee of Imperial Defense.

Military Operations, France and Belgium, 1917.

Vol. I: *The German Retreat to the Hindenburg Line and the Battles of Arras.* London, 1940.

Vol. II: *Messines and Third Ypres (Passchendaele).* London, 1948.

Vol. III: *The Battle of Cambrai.* London, 1948.

Military Operations, Macedonia: From the Spring of 1917 to the End of the War. London, 1935.

The three volumes on British campaigns in France during

1917 deal in part with efforts to develop adequate command arrangements in France. The volume on the Macedonian campaign provides some information on the differing attitudes of the French and the British concerning the scope of operations in that theater.

Les armées françaises dans la grande guerre. France. Ministère de la guerre. Service historique.

Part V: *L'Offensive d'Avril 1917.—Les opérations à objectifs limités (1er Novembre 1916—1er Novembre 1917).*

Part VI: *L'Hiver 1917-1918.—L'Offensive allemande (1er Novembre 1917—18 Juillet 1918).*

Part VIII: *La campagne d'Orient (Dardanelles et Salonique).*

Individual volumes within each Part are cited in the text. Parts V and VI throw some light on the development of the unified command. They also reveal the seriousness of the military situation in France which had so much to do with the impulse to establish the Supreme War Council. The volume on the Macedonian campaign documents the desire of the French to launch a major offensive in the Balkans.

United States Army in the World War. 17 vols. Washington, 1948.

This large collection of printed documents relating to the American Expeditionary Forces in France during World War I is interspersed with brief commentaries. It covers all aspects of American operations. Volume II, *Policy-Forming Documents,* is most useful for the study of American military strategy during the war. It includes many documents dealing with the activities of General Bliss at Versailles. It is the best collection of printed sources on General Pershing's command. Volume III, *Training and Use of American Troops with British and French,* includes valuable information on amalgamation.

E. Memoirs and Published Papers

Amery, L. S., *My Political Life.* 3 vols. London, 1953-1955.

Vol. II: *War and Peace, 1914-1929.* London, 1953.

The author was head of the Political Branch of the British Section at Versailles during World War I. He casts light on the inner history of the controversy between Lloyd George and General Robertson.

Blake, Robert, ed., *The Private Papers of Douglas Haig 1914-1919.* London, 1952.

This collection, principally excerpts from Haig's diary, is useful for an understanding of Haig's role in the formation of British strategy and the political-military strife within the British government.

Bliss, General Tasker H., "The Evolution of the Unified Command," *Foreign Affairs* (December, 1922), I, 1-30.

This article emphasizes the activities of the Supreme War Council in connection with the creation of Foch's command, especially the significance of the General Reserve. It also indicates the nature of American support for the principle of unified command.

Clemenceau, Georges, *Grandeur and Misery of Victory.* New York, 1930.

A memoir which deals largely with Clemenceau's relationships with other war leaders.

Churchill, Winston S., *The World Crisis.* 4 vols. New York, 1923-1929.

Vol. III: *1916-1918.* New York, 1927.

Foch, Ferdinand, *Memoirs of Marshal Foch.* Colonel T. Bentley Mott, trans. Garden City, New York, 1931.

This book indicates the Marshal's attitude toward the Supreme War Council and is useful for the study of the unified command.

Grant, U.S., III, "America's Part in the Supreme War Council," *Records of the Columbia Historical Society* (New York, 1928), XXIX-XXX, 295-340.

Colonel Grant was the secretary of the American Section at Versailles. His account throws light on the institutional characteristics of the American Section and on various personalities including General Bliss. It also discusses those issues which particularly attracted American interest.

Graves, General William S., *America's Siberian Adventure:1918-1920.* New York, 1931.

Graves' memoir gives details of American attempts to implement the highly restrained policy toward intervention developed by President Wilson.

Hankey, Lord (Maurice), *Diplomacy by Conference: Studies in*

Public Affairs 1920-1946. London, 1946.

Hankey was usually present at inter-Allied gatherings during World War I in his capacity as secretary of the British War Cabinet. He comments briefly on the Supreme War Council, which he considers to have been of the greatest importance during 1918.

Harbord, General James G., *The American Army in France, 1917-1919*. Boston, 1936.

Harbord was first Pershing's Chief of Staff and later Commander of the Services of Supply.

House, Edward M., *The Intimate Papers of Colonel House*. Charles Seymour, ed. 4 vols. Boston, 1926-1928.

Vol. III: *Into the World War*. Boston, 1928.

Vol. IV: *The Ending of the War*. Boston, 1928.

Colonel House was the President's principal personal contact with the leaders of the Entente Powers. The focus of the work somewhat exaggerates the importance of House, but comparison with other sources renders *The Intimate Papers* remarkably useful for the study of World War I.

Lansing, Robert, *War Memoirs of Robert Lansing, Secretary of State*. Indianapolis, 1935.

This book consists largely of printed excerpts from memoranda made by the Secretary during his membership in President Wilson's cabinet.

Lloyd George, David, *War Memoirs of David Lloyd George*. 6 vols. Boston, 1933-1937.

Vol. IV: *1917*. Boston, 1934.

Vol. V: *1917-1918*. Boston, 1936.

Vol. VI: *1918*. Boston, 1937.

The Prime Minister's memoirs are useful for British attitudes toward the other members of the Western coalition. The author gives much space to discussions of inter-Allied consultations, in particular the activities of the Supreme War Council. Since much of the commentary is a defense of the Prime Minister's actions, it must be checked against other sources when possible. Much space is given to discussions of strategy and policy.

Lockhart, R. H. Bruce, *British Agent*. New York, 1933.

Lockhart served as an unofficial contact with the Bolsheviks during the early days of the Russian Revolution. His book gives indications of British attitudes toward the Bolsheviks and the attempt to work out a basis of cooperation with them in 1918.

March, General Peyton C., *The Nation at War.* Garden City, New York, 1932.

The memoirs of the wartime Chief of Staff deal mostly with domestic mobilization. He had little to do with grand strategy. The book is interesting chiefly for its accounts of the War Department's operation and relationships with the American Expeditionary Forces.

Maurice, Sir Frederick B., *Lessons of Allied Co-operation: Naval, Military, and Air, 1914-1918.* New York, 1942.

This study is one of the few dealing specifically with inter-Allied cooperation during World War I. The author held the important post of Director of Military Operations in the British War Office during the period of Robertson's tenure as C.I.G.S. The book surveys the development of cooperation. Maurice emphasizes the need for political control of strategy but inveighs against undue political interference with the implementation of general strategy in particular theaters.

Painlevé, Paul, *Comment j'ai nommé Foch et Pétain: La politique de guerre de 1917: Le commandement unique interallié.* Paris, 1924.

This memoir provides information on the French contribution to the creation of the Supreme War Council. Painlevé was Premier of France at the time of the Council's establishment.

Pershing, General John J., *My Experiences in the World War.* 2 vols. New York, 1931.

The Commander-in-Chief's account of the history of the A.E.F. concentrates primarily on the training and employment of the American army in France. He gives a great deal of space to the amalgamation controversy.

Sims, Admiral William S., and Burton J. Hendrick, *The Victory at Sea.* Garden City, New York, 1920.

This book concentrates on the war against the submarines. It includes some information on the initiation and expansion of naval cooperation with the Entente.

Willert, Arthur, *The Road to Safety: A Study in Anglo-American Relations.* London, 1952.

Willert was associated with the British mission to the United

States during World War I. His book throws light on the activities of Sir William Wiseman and the British methods of dealing with the United States government.

II. *Secondary Works*

A. Studies of Special Subjects

Cruttwell, C. R. M. F., *A History of the Great War.* 2nd edn., Oxford, 1936.

Curry, Roy W., *Woodrow Wilson and Far Eastern Policy, 1913-1921.* New York, 1957.

The author devotes a portion of his book to the question of intervention in Siberia.

Edmonds, James E., *A Short History of World War I.* London, 1951.

The author was one of the compilers of the British official history. He is a strong defender of the "western strategy" and takes issue with critics like Liddell Hart who comment adversely on the principle of frontal attacks against well-entrenched forces.

Frothingham, Thomas G., *The Naval History of the Great War.* 3 vols. Cambridge, Massachusetts, 1924-1926.

Vol. III: *The United States in the War, 1917-1918.* Cambridge, Massachusetts, 1926.

George, A. L., and J. L. George, *Woodrow Wilson and Colonel House: A Personality Study.* New York, 1956.

A pioneering attempt to explore the formation of personality and its impact on policy-making. The authors utilize the insights of present-day psychological and sociological studies to advantage.

Kennan, George F., *Soviet-American Relations, 1917-1920.* Princeton, 1956–[in process].

Vol. I: *Russia Leaves the War.* Princeton, 1956.

Vol. II: *The Decision to Intervene.* Princeton, 1958.

The first volume deals with events in Russia from the Bolshevik assumption of power in November 1917 to the Treaty of Brest-Litovsk in March 1918. There is a section on the background of the Allied effort to intervene in Soviet Russia. Volume II concentrates on the process by which the Allies arrived at the decision to launch intervention. It concludes with the departure of the Americans from Russia in the late summer of 1918.

King, Jere C., *Generals and Politicians; Conflict Between France's High Command, Parliament and Government, 1914-1918.* Berkeley, California, 1951.

An excellent study of civil-military relations within France during the First World War.

Kreidberg, M. A., and M. G. Henry, *History of Military Mobilization in the United States Army 1775-1945.* Washington, 1955.

One large section of this exhaustive treatise traces the American mobilization during World War I.

Liddell Hart, Basil H., *The Real War 1914-1918.* Boston, 1918.

A general military history of the war which is strongly critical of Allied strategy and tactics.

Lonergan, Thomas C., *It Might Have Been Lost.* New York, 1929.

A defense of the American refusal to allow the integration of American troops into European armies.

May, Ernest R., "The Development of Political-Military Consultation in the United States," *Political Science Quarterly* (June, 1955), LXX, 161-180.

The author traces the growth of consultative institutions within the American government designed to coordinate national policy and strategy.

McEntee, Girard L., *Military History of the World War.* New York, 1931.

Rudin, Harry R., *Armistice 1918.* New Haven, Connecticut, 1944.

A standard work on the armistice. Long extracts from the official records of the eighth session of the Supreme War Council are in the text.

Seymour, Charles, *American Diplomacy During the World War.* Baltimore, 1934.

A standard work on the subject. It is based largely on the House Papers and printed documents.

Shumate, Thomas Daniel, Jr., "The Allied Supreme War Council, 1917-1918." Unpublished Ph.D. dissertation. University of Virginia, 1952.

This large manuscript deals with the general history of the Supreme War Council. It is based on research in both American and European archives as well as in printed sources and secondary works. It is the best available discussion of the Council.

Unterberger, Betty M., *America's Siberian Expedition, 1918-1920: A Study of National Policy.* Durham, North Carolina, 1956.

This book is the best study of the Siberian episode. The author stresses the threat to American interest and security posed by Japan. Unlike most writers on the subject she takes note of the Supreme War Council's activities.

Warth, Robert D., *The Allies and the Russian Revolution.* Durham, North Carolina, 1954.

A study of the period prior to the Treaty of Brest-Litovsk. The author emphasizes the confusion which attended Allied contacts with the Bolsheviks.

White, John A., *The Siberian Intervention.* Princeton, 1953.

This study stresses the economic motivations which influenced the Allied policy toward Soviet Russia.

Wright, Peter, *At the Supreme War Council.* New York, 1921.

A polemical work defending the establishment of the unified command and critical of Haig and Robertson. Wright was a member of the British Section at Versailles.

B. Biographies.

Baker, Ray Stannard, *Woodrow Wilson: Life and Letters.* 8 vols. New York, 1927-1939.

Vol. VII: *War Leader.* New York, 1939.

Vol. VIII: *Armistice.* New York, 1939.

These volumes include excerpts from the Wilson Papers arranged chronologically for the period of American belligerency.

Bell, Herbert C. F., *Woodrow Wilson and the People.* New York, 1945.

A discerning one-volume biography.

Callwell, Major-General C. E., *Field-Marshal Sir Henry Wilson: His Life and Diaries.* 2 vols. London, 1927.

Sir Henry Wilson was first the British military representative at Versailles and then the British Chief of the Imperial General Staff after the removal of Robertson in February 1918. His diary provides insights into the formation of British strategy and policy during 1918. He helped to develop the British concept of the proposed War Council in 1917.

Cooper, Duff, *Haig*. 2 vols. London, 1936.

A general biography of the Commander-in-Chief of the British Expeditionary Forces in France.

Palmer, Frederick, *Bliss, Peacemaker: The Life and Letters of General Tasker Howard Bliss.* New York, 1934.

This is the authorized biography of Bliss, based primarily on the General's papers now deposited in the Library of Congress.

———, *Newton D. Baker.* 2 vols. New York, 1931.

This is the authorized biography, based on Baker's papers now in the Library of Congress.

Index